Divine
Mystical
Truths

Guide to Joyful Living

Kevin Michael VerKamp

ISBN: 979-8-9887863-0-6 (Hardcover)
ISBN: 979-8-9887863-1-3 (Softcover)
ISBN: 979-8-9887863-2-0 (eBook)

Dedicated to my parents,

In the symphony of my life, your love has been the constant, harmonious melody that has underpinned every note of my existence. Your strength has been my pillar, your wisdom my guiding light, and your sacrifices the silent fuel that has propelled me forward. Your unwavering faith in me has been a reminder of my potential, even when I faltered in my belief. You've taught me the art of resilience, the beauty of kindness, and the power of dreams. This book is a testament to the values you've instilled in me and the nurturing environment you've cultivated. For every word that spills onto these pages, there is a thank you whispered into the universe for you.

And to my wife,

Every word within the pages of this book bears the invisible ink of your support, love, and inspiration. Your unwavering faith in me, your patience during countless late nights, and your ability to bring comfort and clarity when doubts threatened to overshadow, have been the steady compass guiding this journey. Our shared experiences, laughter, and intimate conversations have shaped my perspectives and breathed life into my writing. For being my muse, my sounding board, my sanctuary, and my greatest cheerleader, I am eternally grateful. This book, like every endeavor of my life, is immeasurably richer for your presence.

And to my dear children,

This book is a legacy of wisdom and knowledge, a treasure chest of lessons I hope will guide you as you forge your own paths in life. Each word is imbued with my deepest hopes, my wildest dreams, and my profound love for you. In this labor of love, may you find a compass to navigate the vast oceans of life, a beacon to illuminate your darkest nights, and a testament to the power of perseverance and the resilience of the human spirit. May these words inspire you to dream boldly, love deeply, and live fully. In you I see the promise of the future, and the very best of what I could ever aspire to be.

Chapter Index

Contents

Prologue

As I put pen to paper to begin this special journey, I am filled with an immense sense of love and a profound desire to share with you the wisdom I've gathered throughout my life. This book is more than a mere collection of thoughts and reflections, it's a legacy of understanding, a treasury of insights, and a map of life lessons, born out of love and passed down to you.

Life is a rich tapestry, woven with countless threads of experiences, emotions, relationships, and discoveries. It is a journey marked by an endless interplay of joys and sorrows, triumphs and trials, beginnings and endings. Yet amid this complex dance of existence, there remain enduring truths, timeless wisdoms, and universal lessons that light our path and guide our steps. These are the lessons I wish to share with you within these pages.

From understanding the nature of love and friendship, the importance of self-knowledge and the beauty of existence, to grappling with concepts such as pain, death, and the power of words, I have attempted to explore the vast landscape of life. This is not a book of absolutes or final answers, but rather, a conversation, a shared exploration, a series of heartfelt reflections.

Through reflections on passion and reason, teaching and learning, the nature of good and evil, time, and the intricacies of religious belief, these chapters aim to stir your thoughts, prompt your questions, and nurture your understanding. They are invitations to ponder, to explore, to journey deeper into the heart of life.

As you traverse these pages, I hope you find comfort in knowing that you are not alone in your questions, your fears, or your hopes. Like countless others before you, you are part of a shared human journey, a grand cosmic dance. And it's in this shared journey, in this dance, that we find connections, understandings, and meaning.

These writings are born from love and they are intended to serve as a beacon for you in the vast sea of life. Yet, this book is just a starting point. It is your journey, your quest, your adventure to undertake. The wisdom offered here is meant to be a companion, not a compass. Your path will be unique to you, guided by your experiences, your insights, your truth.

As you navigate through life, remember, at its core, it's love that connects us, love that enriches us, and love that ultimately defines our lives. It's the most essential wisdom I can bestow upon you: Love deeply, live authentically, and seek to understand both the world around you and the world within you.

In this collection of reflections, I hope you find solace, understanding, and guidance. And as you embark on your journey through life, may these Divine Mystical Truths illuminate your path, enrich your experiences, and ultimately, guide you towards a life filled with love, wisdom, and profound peace.

Kevin Michael VerKamp

Essence of Love

Love is the lifeblood of existence, the thread that weaves together the tapestry of life. It's the very essence of who we are, the deepest yearning of our hearts.

Love is not merely a feeling, but a way of being. It's about seeing the beauty in each other, recognizing the interconnectedness of all life, cherishing the inherent worth of every being. It's about embracing kindness, fostering understanding, promoting peace.

Love is what compels us to lift each other up, to support each other in times of need, to celebrate each other's joys. It's what motivates us to act with compassion, to speak with kindness, to live with integrity. It's what drives us to build bridges, to mend fences, to heal wounds.

True love isn't always easy. It calls us to look beyond our differences, to let go of our prejudices, to forgive our transgressions. It asks us to be patient, to be selfless, to be brave. It invites us to be vulnerable, to be open, to be authentic.

Love is not just about loving others, but also about loving ourselves. It's about acknowledging our worth, nurturing our growth, honoring our journey. It's about embracing our strengths, accepting our weaknesses, celebrating our uniqueness.

True love, in essence, is unconditional. It doesn't judge, it doesn't discriminate, it doesn't expect. It simply is. It's a flame that illuminates, a melody that harmonizes, a river that flows. It's the sun that warms, the moon that guides, the star that shines.

Love deeply, love truly, love unconditionally. Love yourself, love each other, love the world. Let love guide your actions, inspire your words, shape your life. For love, in all its beauty and power, is the ultimate truth, the highest wisdom, the grandest journey. It's the key to understanding, the path to peace, the gateway to joy.

Love is our true nature, our highest calling, our deepest purpose. Embrace it, nurture it, live it. For in love, we find our true selves, we discover our shared humanity, we realize our collective destiny. Love, in its purest form, is the essence of life, the heart of existence, the soul of the universe. Love, truly, is all there is.

Dual Nature of Desires

Desires, like a river, are a natural and integral part of our human existence. They flow through the landscape of our lives, shaping our paths, and propelling us forward. They give us motivation, fuel our dreams, and bring color and passion to our lives. Yet, like a river, if unchecked or unguided, desires can overflow their banks, causing chaos and confusion.

Desires can manifest in countless ways: for material possessions, recognition, power, love, peace, or even enlightenment. They are born from our aspirations, our needs, and our longing for fulfillment. In many ways, they define our pursuits and give meaning to our actions.

But desires are a double-edged sword. They can both inspire us and enslave us. When harnessed correctly, desires can lead to motivation, innovation, and fulfillment. They can push us to strive, to grow, and to transcend our limitations. Yet, unchecked or unfulfilled desires can also lead to dissatisfaction, frustration, and even suffering.

The key, therefore, lies not in the suppression of desires, but in their understanding and mindful management. It requires self-awareness to discern between desires that serve us and those that do not. It calls for wisdom to navigate the delicate balance between ambition and contentment.

Healthy desires can propel us on a path of continuous learning, self-improvement, and positive impact. They encourage us to create, to achieve, and to contribute. Conversely, desires rooted in greed, envy, or insecurity often lead to stress, disappointment, and conflict.

Learning to navigate our desires also means understanding that the fulfilment of desire is not an endpoint but a part of the journey. The joy derived from desire is often found not just in attainment, but in the pursuit itself, in the growth that it fosters, and in the person we become along the way.

Use your desires as a compass guiding you towards growth, fulfillment, and contribution, but do not let them become chains that bind you. Remember, desires are part of the journey, not the destination. They are tools for our evolution, not the measure of our worth.

Waves of Emotion

Emotions are the vibrant colors on the canvas of our lives, imbuing our experiences with shades of joy, sorrow, fear, anger, love, and myriad other feelings. They form an integral part of our human existence, guiding our interactions, shaping our perceptions, and influencing our decisions.

Each emotion we experience serves a unique purpose. Joy uplifts us, fueling our energy and passion. Sadness allows us to acknowledge our pain, initiating healing and growth. Fear protects us, alerting us to danger and preparing us for action. Anger signals injustice, spurring us to defend ourselves or our values. Love binds us together, fostering connection and empathy.

However, emotions are not always comfortable to experience. They can be intense, overwhelming, and sometimes even seemingly contradictory. It is in these moments of discomfort, though, that emotions offer their greatest insights. They act as signals, pointing to areas within ourselves that need attention, healing, or transformation.

Yet, it's important to understand that emotions are transient. Like waves on an ocean, they come and go, each wave unique in its shape, size, and impact. No matter how intense the emotion may be, it will pass, giving way to another, just as a wave recedes, making way for the next.

To navigate the seas of our emotions effectively, mindfulness is key. It involves observing our feelings without judgment, allowing them to exist without attempting to suppress or amplify them. Mindfulness asks us to sit with our emotions, to understand their origins, their implications, and what they are trying to communicate.

Remember, emotions are not inherently good or bad; they simply are. Each one has a role to play and a lesson to impart. They are not weaknesses but signals, not the entirety of our experience but components of it. We are not our emotions, but we experience them, and through this experience, we understand ourselves and our world more deeply.

Emotions are integral parts of your human experiences. Listen to their wisdom, learn from their lessons, and let them guide you on your journey of self-discovery. For it is through our emotions that we connect, not only with ourselves but also with the world around us. It is through emotions that we truly live.

Less is More

Simplicity, often overshadowed by the allure of complexity, holds within it a depth and beauty that can bring profound peace and fulfillment. It is a gentle beckoning towards a life uncluttered by excess, a life that prioritizes quality over quantity, meaning over multiplicity.

In its essence, simplicity is about stripping away the unnecessary, about identifying what truly matters and letting go of what does not. It's about making room for what enriches our lives and discarding what burdens them. This can apply to our material possessions, our relationships, our goals, our habits, and even our thoughts.

The pursuit of simplicity does not mean leading an ascetic life or rejecting progress and ambition. Instead, it encourages us to be mindful of our choices, to discern between need and want, to choose intention over impulse. Simplicity invites us to be deliberate in our actions, to ensure that what we do, say, and think contributes to our well-being and aligns with our values.

Simplicity also fosters clarity. In a world overloaded with information, options, and distractions, simplicity helps us cut through the noise, focus on our objectives, and align our actions accordingly. It serves as a compass, guiding us towards actions and choices that resonate with our core selves.

Moreover, simplicity nurtures peace and contentment. It frees us from the exhausting pursuit of more, allowing us to find joy and fulfillment in what we already have.

Embracing simplicity is akin to treading a path lined with wisdom and grace. It is a journey of understanding that true abundance is not about having more, but about needing less. It's about realizing that the most beautiful and meaningful moments often reside not in the grandeur, but in the simple, the mundane, the ordinary.

In a world that often equates complexity with sophistication and success, let us not forget the inherent power and elegance of simplicity. For in simplicity, we find clarity, peace, and an appreciation for life's essential joys.

Touch of Kindness

Kindness, a simple yet profound expression of human goodwill, is a bridge connecting hearts and fostering understanding. It is a universal language transcending boundaries of culture, religion, and social status, imbued with the power to transform lives and mend divides.

Kindness begins with the recognition of our shared humanity, acknowledging that we are all on a journey, filled with joys and sorrows, hopes and fears. It stems from empathy, understanding that beneath our unique stories and individual experiences, we all seek happiness and yearn to avoid suffering.

In its purest form, kindness is selfless. It expects nothing in return. It's a gift of the heart, given freely, often finding expression in simple acts. A warm smile, a gentle word, a thoughtful gesture – these are all threads in the tapestry of kindness that we weave in our lives and the lives of others.

Kindness not only impacts the receiver, but also enriches the giver. It cultivates inner peace, fosters gratitude, and nurtures a sense of interconnectedness. By extending kindness to others, we nurture it within ourselves, creating a cycle of goodwill that can reverberate through our communities.

Kindness must also extend inward. Self-kindness, often overlooked, is the foundation upon which all other kindness is built. It involves treating ourselves with the same compassion and understanding we offer others. It's about acknowledging our flaws without judgment, extending patience to our mistakes, and granting ourselves the same gentleness we provide to others.

In a world where harshness and criticism can often prevail, kindness serves as a beacon of hope. It reminds us of the potential for goodness in each interaction, the possibility for connection in each encounter. It invites us to look past differences and disagreements, to see the inherent worth in every individual.

The beauty of kindness is in its accessibility. It requires no special skills or resources, only an open heart and a willingness to act. It's a choice we can make in every moment, an opportunity to add a touch of warmth to the world around us.

Kindness is a light we can all shine, a song we can all sing, a gift we can all give.

Accept Everything with Love

Accepting everything with love is a powerful philosophy that can profoundly transform our relationship with life. It's an invitation to navigate the world with an open heart and a receptive mind, to embrace every experience as part of our journey, and to perceive every encounter as an opportunity for growth and learning.

Accepting everything with love means letting go of resistance and judgment. It's about saying 'yes' to life in all its hues - the joyous and the challenging, the beautiful and the seemingly ugly, the known and the mysterious. This doesn't imply passivity or resignation, but a conscious choice to engage with reality as it is, not as we wish it to be.

This principle becomes particularly potent in the face of adversity. Pain, loss, disappointment, and change are inevitable aspects of human existence. Accepting these with love doesn't diminish their difficulty, but it does offer a lens of compassion and understanding that can alleviate suffering. It allows us to hold our pain tenderly, to learn from it, and to harness it for our evolution.

Accepting others with love, too, is a vital aspect of this philosophy. Each individual is a complex tapestry of strengths, weaknesses, dreams, fears, triumphs, and struggles. When we accept others with love, we acknowledge their humanity in all its brilliance and imperfection. We practice empathy, kindness, and respect. We cultivate harmonious relationships and contribute to a more compassionate world.

Accepting ourselves with love is perhaps the most transformative application of this principle. We often subject ourselves to harsh judgment, unrealistic expectations, and conditional self-worth. By lovingly accepting ourselves - our abilities, our shortcomings, our aspirations, our mistakes - we foster self-esteem, self-compassion, and inner peace. We empower ourselves to grow, not from a place of inadequacy, but from a place of self-love.

Ultimately, accepting everything with love is a path to profound wisdom. It teaches us to honor life in all its complexity, to find beauty in the mundane, strength in adversity, and joy in the simple act of being. It enables us to navigate life with grace, resilience, and an open heart, embracing the journey in all its multifaceted glory.

Power of Ignorance

Ignorance, often viewed negatively, is a universal human condition we all grapple with. It represents the spaces in our understanding, the yet-to-be-explored territories of our knowledge and perception. It's the acknowledgement that despite our advancements and experiences, there is still so much we don't know.

In one perspective, ignorance is akin to darkness. It can limit our vision, obscure our path, and influence our decisions and actions in ways that may not serve us or others well. This form of ignorance, particularly when coupled with arrogance or denial, can lead to misunderstanding, prejudice, and harm.

Ignorance need not be viewed solely as a liability. It can also serve as a starting point for learning and growth. Acknowledging our ignorance, admitting that there are things we don't know or understand, is the first step towards seeking knowledge and wisdom. It is the spark that ignites the flame of curiosity, the prompt that drives us to question, explore, and learn.

This transformative process requires humility and courage. It involves setting aside our preconceived notions and biases, being open to new perspectives, and valuing the quest for truth over the comfort of assumed understanding. It requires the bravery to step into the unknown, to question even our most deeply held beliefs, and to continuously refine our understanding based on new information and experiences.

But even as we strive to overcome ignorance, it's crucial to remember that it's impossible to know everything. Some mysteries of the universe may forever remain beyond our grasp. And that's okay. This acceptance can instill in us a sense of humility, an appreciation for the vastness of existence, and a respect for the diverse perspectives and experiences of others.

In this light, ignorance is not a personal failing, but a part of the human condition. It's an invitation to learn, grow, and connect with others. It's a reminder of the vastness of the universe and the limitlessness of potential understanding. Seen this way, ignorance can serve not as a barrier, but as a catalyst for lifelong learning, curiosity, and growth.

Cultivating Persistence

Persistence, often characterized by steadfastness and tenacity, is the act of persevering in the face of adversity, challenge, and even failure. It is a fundamental trait that fuels the pursuit of our dreams, the accomplishment of our goals, and the overcoming of obstacles that stand in our way.

The essence of persistence is not about never falling or never failing, but rather about the ability to rise each time we fall, to learn from each failure we encounter, and to continue moving forward. It's about acknowledging setbacks as part of the journey and recognizing that the road to success is often winding, steep, and filled with unexpected detours.

Persistence is closely intertwined with resilience and patience. It involves resilience to endure the challenges and hardships we face, and patience to understand that meaningful achievements take time to unfold. It's about maintaining our focus and determination, even when progress is slow and our goals seem distant.

Persistence is not about stubbornly clinging to a path that is clearly not serving us. There's wisdom in knowing when to pivot, when to reassess our approach, and when to let go of goals that no longer align with our values or aspirations. Thus, effective persistence also involves adaptability and flexibility. It's about being committed to our journey, but open to changing our path as needed.

Cultivating persistence starts with fostering a growth mindset, viewing challenges as opportunities for learning rather than as insurmountable barriers. It involves developing self-confidence and believing in our ability to overcome obstacles. It requires setting clear and meaningful goals, maintaining a positive attitude, and seeking support when needed.

In a world where success is often glamorized and failure is feared, it's essential to remember that every accomplished individual, every thriving organization, has faced setbacks and failures along their journey. It is persistence, the courage to continue despite these setbacks, that often makes the difference between dreams realized and dreams abandoned.

The strength of persistence is not merely about reaching our destination, but also about the person we become, the skills we develop, and the wisdom we gain along the way. Let persistence be your compass, guiding you through the challenges and towards the realization of your dreams.

Habit Loop

Habit is a powerful force that shapes our lives in subtle yet significant ways. They are the automatic patterns of behavior, thought, and emotion that arise through repeated action and exposure, becoming ingrained in our daily routines and ways of thinking. Habits are the unnoticed architects of our lives, quietly building and shaping our days and, ultimately, our destinies.

Consider the simplicity of a single habit. A habit like drinking a glass of water first thing in the morning may seem insignificant on its own. Yet, when sustained over time, it contributes to our hydration, metabolism, and overall health. It is the accumulative effect of small habits, repeated day in and day out, that leads to significant changes and outcomes in our lives.

Habits are not only about action, they also involve our ways of thinking and feeling. For example, a habitual pattern of negative thinking can shape our outlook on life, affecting our mood, relationships, and even our mental health. Cultivating positive thinking habits can enhance our wellbeing, resilience, and interactions with others.

Habits, once formed, are not always easy to change. Our brains naturally gravitate towards efficiency, defaulting to established patterns and routines. That's why breaking old habits or forming new ones can be challenging. It requires effort, patience, and consistency. But with conscious intent, understanding of the habit loop (cue, routine, reward), and employing strategies such as habit stacking and environmental design, we can harness the power of habits to serve our goals and wellbeing.

It's important to note that not all habits serve us well. Some, like excessive consumption of unhealthy food or procrastination, can have negative impacts on our lives. Recognizing and modifying these habits is an essential part of personal growth and self-improvement.

Habits are the tools of transformation. They are the small, often unnoticed steps that, when taken consistently, lead us towards the realization of our aspirations. They are proof that change does not always require grand gestures or dramatic shifts. Sometimes, all it takes is the repeated practice of small, positive habits. The key lies in identifying the habits that serve our goals and nurturing them with intention and consistency.

Navigating Doubt

Doubt, a state of uncertainty or a lack of conviction, is a universal human experience that plays a complex and multifaceted role in our lives. It is often perceived negatively, as it can trigger feelings of confusion, discomfort, and fear. However, when approached with openness and curiosity, doubt can serve as a valuable catalyst for growth, innovation, and deeper understanding.

At its core, doubt pushes us to question, to reassess, and to critically evaluate our beliefs, decisions, and actions. It urges us to test the validity of our assumptions and to challenge the status quo. In this context, doubt can stimulate intellectual growth and foster a mindset of continuous learning. It can lead to the discarding of outdated beliefs and the embracing of new perspectives, paving the way for personal transformation and societal progress.

Doubt also plays a crucial role in decision-making. It prompts us to pause, reflect, gather more information, and weigh the potential outcomes before taking action. It encourages us to be more thoughtful, careful, and deliberate in our choices, thereby potentially reducing mistakes and enhancing the quality of our decisions.

It's important to differentiate between constructive doubt and paralyzing doubt. Constructive doubt encourages questioning and facilitates learning and growth, while paralyzing doubt can lead to indecision, inaction, and a lack of self-confidence. When doubt becomes chronic and all-consuming, it can hinder our progress and diminish our wellbeing. Thus, learning to navigate doubt effectively is a key aspect of emotional intelligence and resilience.

To manage doubt constructively, we can cultivate a mindset that embraces uncertainty as an opportunity for learning and growth. We can develop critical thinking skills to evaluate our doubts objectively and make well-informed decisions. We can practice mindfulness to stay grounded in the present and reduce anxiety about the unknown. And we can foster self-compassion to accept our doubts without self-judgment, recognizing that it's a part of the human experience.

Doubt is not an enemy to be feared, but rather a companion on our journey of growth and discovery. It invites us to question, to explore, and to strive for deeper understanding. When navigated with awareness and skill, doubt can serve as a powerful tool for learning, growth, and positive change.

Adaptability

Adaptability is the capacity to adjust and thrive in the face of change, uncertainty, and new circumstances. It is a vital quality in our rapidly evolving world, where the pace of technological progress, societal transformation, and environmental shifts often outstrips our ability to predict what lies ahead. Adaptability empowers us not just to survive, but to navigate and leverage the winds of change to our advantage.

Adaptability is about flexibility, openness, and resilience. It is the willingness to let go of old ways of thinking and doing, the readiness to embrace new ideas and approaches, and the resilience to bounce back from challenges and setbacks. It involves learning from our experiences, making adjustments based on our learnings, and developing new strategies to better handle future changes.

Adaptability also includes cognitive flexibility, which refers to our ability to switch between different concepts, to consider multiple perspectives, and to apply different thinking strategies to solve problems. It aids us in navigating complex situations, fosters creativity and innovation, and enables us to respond effectively to unexpected changes.

Adaptability does not mean constant change or lack of consistency. It's not about abandoning our principles, values, or long-term goals. Rather, it's about altering our approach and tactics as needed while keeping our core values and objectives intact. It's about being steadfast in our purpose, but flexible in our methods.

Cultivating adaptability involves developing a growth mindset, which sees challenges as opportunities for learning and growth rather than threats. It requires enhancing our emotional intelligence to manage our emotions and respond effectively to change. It also involves fostering resilience, developing problem-solving skills, and seeking diverse experiences that broaden our perspective and enhance our capacity to handle change.

In a world marked by constant change, adaptability is not just a useful skill, but a necessary one. It is the key to our continued growth, learning, and evolution. It empowers us to navigate the unpredictable currents of life with grace and agility, turning the uncertainties of change into opportunities for growth and transformation.

Compassion's Echo of Love

Compassion, a beacon of light in the midst of human suffering, is an innate ability to understand and empathize with the pain of others and a desire to alleviate it. It's an expression of the interconnectedness of all beings, a realization that the sufferings and joys of one can reverberate in the hearts of many.

Compassion encourages us to look beyond the surface, beyond the walls people build around themselves, to see their inherent vulnerability and humanity. It asks us to acknowledge the shared experience of being human, complete with all its trials and tribulations, joys and sorrows.

The act of compassion is not merely feeling sorry for someone; it's acknowledging their pain as if it were your own and actively seeking to comfort and help. Compassion moves us to reach out, to extend a hand, to offer a word of kindness, or to simply be present. It is an act of love, of empathy, of profound understanding.

Compassion also extends to oneself. It asks us to treat ourselves with the same kindness and understanding we offer others. In recognizing our own struggles and treating ourselves gently, we can better understand and empathize with the struggles of others.

Interestingly, compassion benefits not only the receiver but also the giver. It can bring a sense of fulfillment and inner peace, knowing that we have eased someone's burden, even if only slightly. It can foster a sense of common humanity, strengthening our connections with others.

Compassion is not always easy. It requires courage and strength to lean into discomfort, to face the suffering of others, and our own. Yet, it is in these moments of challenge that compassion shines brightest, illuminating the path toward understanding, connection, and healing.

In a world often divided by differences, compassion is a bridge that unites us. It is a reminder of the fundamental human capacity for kindness and empathy. As we navigate through life, may we always carry with us the beacon of compassion, casting its gentle light on the shadows of suffering, bringing hope, comfort, and connection.

Alone, Not Lonely

Solitude is often mistaken as a mere absence of company, a state of loneliness. But in reality, solitude is far from loneliness. It is a state of being that allows one to be fully present with oneself. It is an opportunity for introspection, reflection, and personal growth.

Solitude provides a space for you to explore the depths of your thoughts and emotions without distraction. It is a silent dialogue with oneself, a journey into the innermost chambers of your heart. Solitude gives you the chance to listen to your inner voice, which is often drowned out by the noise and demands of the outside world.

In the quietude of solitude, one can confront their fears, aspirations, regrets, and joys. Here, we have the freedom to be completely honest with ourselves. This candid introspection can lead to profound self-understanding and self-awareness, enabling us to recognize our strengths, weaknesses, and areas for growth.

Solitude provides a unique opportunity to cultivate resilience. It teaches us to be comfortable in our own company, to find peace within ourselves, and to enjoy our own thoughts and dreams. It shows us that we are not defined by the presence of others, but by our own values, actions, and character.

Solitude isn't about isolating oneself from the world; it is about developing a deeper understanding of oneself so that one can engage with the world more authentically. It's about creating a healthy relationship with oneself, which in turn fosters healthier relationships with others.

In this fast-paced, interconnected world, moments of solitude can be rare, but their value is immeasurable. They offer a reprieve from the relentless speed of life, a chance to slow down, to reflect, and to reconnect with ourselves.

Embrace solitude. Bask in its quiet. Listen to its whisper. Dance to its rhythm. It is in solitude that you can truly meet yourself, with all your complexities, eccentricities, and beautiful imperfections. In solitude, you may discover that the companion you've been seeking has been with you all along.

Value of Silence

Silence, often overlooked in the rush and noise of our busy lives, holds profound value. It is not merely the absence of sound, but a profound state of being, a space for introspection, a gateway to deeper understanding, and a canvas on which the subtle harmonies of life can be appreciated.

In silence, we find a retreat from the clamor of the external world. Here, we can listen to the whisperings of our innermost thoughts, we can decipher the rhythm of our emotions, we can tune into the music of our hearts. Silence allows us to detach ourselves from the incessant chatter of our minds and brings us face to face with our authentic selves.

Silence is a mirror that reflects our inner state with unabashed honesty. It invites introspection, facilitating a dialogue with our own consciousness. In silence, we can confront our fears, our desires, our joys, and our sorrows. It is the birthplace of self-awareness, fostering a deeper understanding of our own motivations, actions, and reactions.

Silence also cultivates mindfulness. In the quiet, we become more attuned to the present moment. We become more sensitive to the world around us—the scent of the rain-soaked earth, the delicate rustling of leaves in the wind, the taste of the air on our tongues. The world comes alive in a whole new way, and we find beauty in details previously unnoticed.

Silence is a teacher, a healer, a philosopher. It gives us the space to absorb, to contemplate, and to grow. It teaches us patience and cultivates resilience. It heals by providing us with the space to process our experiences, to let go of what no longer serves us, and to welcome new thoughts and perspectives.

Remember that silence need not be feared or considered as empty. It is a sanctuary of peace, a reservoir of wisdom, and an intimate dialogue with the self. It is in silence that we hear the most profound truths, that we touch the deepest parts of our being, and that we connect with the essence of life itself.

Take a moment. Breathe. Embrace the silence. Listen. What you hear might surprise you, enlighten you, or transform you. After all, silence isn't empty; it is full of answers.

Unveiling Wisdom

Wisdom - it is not simply the accumulation of knowledge, the collection of facts, or the mastering of skills. It is an entity far more complex, far more profound. Wisdom is an expansive landscape, a deep ocean, an infinite cosmos in itself. It is an understanding that seeps into the marrow of your bones, a truth that echoes in the chambers of your heart. It stems not from memorized words or learned logic, but from a deep well of empathy and insight within us.

At its core, wisdom is the embodiment of compassion, kindness, and love, an unwavering commitment to these guiding stars. This is a wisdom not confined to the intellect, a wisdom not chained by the limitations of the human mind. It's a wisdom that runs deep, swirling in the undercurrents of our very being.

True wisdom illuminates the inherent worth in each individual, the invisible threads of connection between us all. It teaches us to extend to others the same respect, the same kindness, and the same love that we would wish upon ourselves. This profound understanding allows us to transcend the boundaries of our own selves, inviting us to see the world through another's eyes, to feel their joy as our joy, their pain as our pain.

The wise do not stand in judgement based on superficial appearances, nor do they allow themselves to be swayed by the transient whims of ego, fear, or anger. They understand that these are fleeting shadows, not reflective of our true nature. Instead, they approach the world around them with an open mind and an open heart. Their interactions are painted with the colours of compassion and understanding, their words resonating with the harmony of empathy and respect.

To be wise is to immerse oneself in the river of life, understanding its ebbs and flows, its calm and turbulence. It is to observe the world with eyes unclouded, to hear its symphony with ears untainted by prejudice. It is to navigate through the journey of existence with an anchored compass, pointing always towards love and kindness.

Such is the essence of wisdom – an intangible yet undeniable force that shapes our thoughts, fuels our actions, and defines our humanity. This wisdom lays the foundation for a life of purpose, fulfillment, and peace. It is the beacon guiding us through the darkness, the steady hand leading us through the storm. Embrace this wisdom, and watch as your life unfolds into a beautiful tapestry of understanding, compassion, and profound love.

Sacred Union of Marriage

It's a journey of two souls, embarking on a shared adventure, promising to accompany each other through life's peaks and valleys. It's more than a contract or an institution, it's a bond of love, a commitment of hearts, a union of spirits.

Marriage isn't about finding someone to complete you, but about joining hands with someone who encourages you to become the fullest, truest version of yourself. It's about nurturing each other's growth, honoring each other's individuality, cherishing each other's dreams.

In a marriage, you promise to be each other's strength in weakness, light in darkness, peace in chaos. You commit to bear each other's burdens, to share in each other's joys, to walk together through life's many seasons. It's a pledge of companionship, a vow of unity, a testament of love.

A successful marriage is not one without challenges, but one that uses these challenges to deepen understanding, to foster growth, to strengthen bonds. It's about seeing disagreements not as battles to be won, but as opportunities for growth. It's about viewing differences not as divisions, but as complements that enrich the tapestry of your shared life.

Marriage calls for patience, understanding, and forgiveness... Requiring courage to be vulnerable, humility to admit mistakes, generosity to forgive. It demands the wisdom to choose your battles, the strength to weather storms, the resolve to stay the course.

Love is the foundation of marriage, but it's the daily acts of kindness, the shared moments of joy, the mutual respect, and the unwavering commitment that keep this foundation strong. It's about choosing each other, every day, in every situation, in every moment.

As you embark on the journey of marriage, do so with love, with commitment, with kindness. Cherish each other, support each other, grow together. Honor the bond you share, value the love you hold, celebrate the journey you're on.

Marriage, in its truest sense, is a beautiful journey, a shared adventure, a dance of love. It's the joining of two paths, the meeting of two hearts, the union of two souls. It's a testament of love, a celebration of commitment, a manifestation of unity. Embrace it, cherish it, honor it. For in marriage, we find companionship, we experience love, we discover unity.

Nurturing Children

Children are the vibrant brushstrokes on the canvas of life, the joyful melodies in the symphony of existence. They embody the purity of love, the innocence of belief, and the boundless potential of growth.

Children are not only the future of our world but also the guardians of its wonder. In their curiosity, they remind us of the joy of discovery. In their playfulness, they teach us the beauty of spontaneity. In their authenticity, they show us the value of being true to oneself.

To look into the eyes of a child is to glimpse into the heart of possibility. It's to be reminded that each of us, regardless of age or experience, holds within us an unquenchable spark of potential. It's to remember that life is not merely about arriving at a destination, but also about cherishing the journey.

As we guide our children through life, we must remember that they are not merely vessels to be filled, but fires to be kindled. Our role is not to shape them in our image, but to support them in becoming their unique, authentic selves. It's to provide them with roots to ground them and wings to let them fly.

Teach them, certainly, but also learn from them. Be their guide, but also their companion. Show them the way, but also walk with them. Help them to understand the world, but also let them discover it for themselves.

Encourage them to dream, to explore, to question, to create. Nurture their curiosity, foster their imagination, celebrate their individuality. Show them the value of kindness, the power of love, the beauty of life. Above all, let them know that they are loved, cherished, valued for who they are.

Children, in essence, are life's way of reminding us of the beauty of new beginnings, the wonder of growth, and the joy of discovery. In their innocence, they remind us of what truly matters. In their simplicity, they teach us about the essence of life.

So, love them, cherish them, guide them. Learn from them, grow with them, journey with them. For in our children, we see the hope of tomorrow, the joy of today, and the promise of a brighter future.

Accepting Fear

Fear is an emotion, a primal and universal one, deeply woven into the fabric of our existence. It's an intricate dance of mind and body, an ancient call-and-response that exists to protect us. Fear is, in essence, a survival mechanism, designed to alert us to perceived threats and prepare us for potential danger.

At the heart of fear, you will find a powerful paradox. Fear can be a jailer, locking us in the confines of our comfort zones, preventing growth and exploration. Yet, it can also be a teacher, a guiding light leading us toward understanding, resilience, and ultimately, courage.

To understand fear is to acknowledge its dual nature. It can trigger our most primal instincts, our fight or flight responses, causing us to act impulsively, irrationally. It can cloud our judgement, impede our progress and entrap us in a cycle of anxiety and doubt. This is the constricting, limiting aspect of fear.

But fear also has the power to clarify, to illuminate. It can force us to confront the very barriers within ourselves that inhibit our growth. It urges us to examine and question, to seek answers and solutions. Each time we face our fears, we step further into knowledge and self-awareness. Through this lens, fear becomes an instrument of enlightenment.

Overcoming fear doesn't mean to eradicate it, for that is not only impossible but also unwise. Fear is a part of us, a component of our human programming. Instead, the journey involves learning to understand our fears, to negotiate with them, to glean wisdom from them, and to build resilience against the paralyzing grip they can often hold over us.

The essence of fear is a question, a what-if. What if I fail? What if I get hurt? What if I'm not enough? By leaning into these questions, we discover a path towards growth and self-understanding. Each fear faced, each what-if answered, is a step towards a more authentic and courageous self.

In the dance with fear, each of us has the capacity to lead. To do so, we must learn to see fear not as an insurmountable obstacle, but as a challenge to be met, a question to be answered, a teacher to learn from. This shift in perspective, while not easy, is a transformative step on the path of growth, resilience, and freedom.

Time and Patience

Patience is a virtue that's deeply intertwined with our understanding of time, our reactions to circumstances, and our relationships with others and ourselves. It is the ability to tolerate delay, endure hardship, and persevere in the face of adversity without frustration or despair. It is a quality that can bring peace, clarity, and strength in times of challenge and uncertainty.

Patience is also about acceptance. It's about acknowledging and accepting the nature of time and the realities of life, understanding that not all things can or should happen immediately, that growth often requires time, and that challenges and delays are an integral part of our journey.

Patience is also linked to our emotional intelligence. It requires managing our emotions effectively, particularly negative ones like anger, frustration, and anxiety. When we practice patience, we choose understanding over judgment, composure over agitation, and long-term rewards over immediate gratification.

Patience is deeply connected to resilience. It empowers us to withstand life's trials with fortitude and grace, to persist in the face of setbacks, and to remain hopeful in times of adversity. It gives us the strength to endure, to keep going, and to hold onto our dreams, even when the going gets tough.

In relationships, patience enables us to be more understanding and forgiving towards others. It allows us to listen more deeply, respond more thoughtfully, and handle conflicts more effectively. It fosters empathy, compassion, and deeper connections.

Cultivating patience involves developing a mindful, present-focused perspective. It requires recognizing and challenging our impulses for immediacy, our tendencies to react rather than respond, and our patterns of resistance towards delay or hardship. Practice acceptance, manage your emotions, and develope resilience.

In a world of fast-paced change and instant gratification, patience can seem out of place. Yet, it is perhaps more important now than ever. For patience is not just about waiting; it's about how we wait, with grace, understanding, and resilience. It's about transforming the process of waiting from a source of stress into an opportunity for growth, learning, and self-improvement. It is a quiet strength that can guide us through life with greater peace, wisdom, and fulfillment.

Aging and Growing Old

Aging, a journey shared by all of humanity, is a topic that fosters both reflection and celebration. It is a process that brings a wisdom that youth cannot grasp, and challenges that call for adaptability and resilience.

As we age, our life becomes a book, each decade a chapter filled with triumphs, failures, moments of love, heartache, clarity, and confusion. Aging offers a wisdom that understands time's fleeting nature, the ebb and flow of life, and the value of simple moments. It helps us appreciate the joy of loved ones and the tranquility within serenity.

Yet, aging also mirrors our vulnerabilities and fears, a reminder of our mortality. It confronts us with our physical limitations and changes in our bodies. Sometimes it feels like a series of losses—of youth, vitality, and for some, purpose. These challenges, however, provide an opportunity to cultivate resilience, inner strength, and a deeper sense of compassion.

Aging highlights the importance of relationships and companionship, underscoring that, while our journey of aging is personal, it need not be solitary. The bonds of friendship and love often gain more significance as we grow older.

Each wrinkle and gray hair is a testament to a life lived, a challenge overcome, a joy celebrated, a loss grieved. Aging is more than an external process; it's a profound internal journey.

Our perception of aging plays a significant role in how we experience it. If we view it only as a decline, we may miss the chance to fully appreciate the depth and breadth of the journey. But if we can perceive aging as a natural, essential part of the human experience, filled with opportunities for growth, understanding, and fulfillment, then growing old becomes less about loss and more about gain—gain of wisdom, depth, self-understanding, and, hopefully, contentment.

Aging is an art—the art of embracing change, accepting oneself, finding purpose, and cultivating a legacy. It's about learning to navigate the delicate balance between holding on and letting go, and through this dance, we uncover the profound aspects of what it truly means to be human.

Harmony with Nature

Nature, in its purest form, is an orchestra of interconnected rhythms, a testament to the profound harmony of life. It is the original maestro, conducting an eternal symphony, inviting all creatures to partake in its melodic celebration.

Consider the vast forests, where towering trees reach skyward, their leaves rustling like whispered secrets in the wind. They are ancient custodians, offering shelter and sustenance to countless organisms, forming a web of life as intricate as it is resilient. The rivers, coursing across landscapes, carry life-giving water, shaping the terrain as they go, carving valleys, creating plains. They serve as arteries of the planet, perpetuating the cycle of life.

The grandeur of mountains and the humble rustle of grass in the wind are but verses in the poetry of nature. Every sunrise, every sunset, every delicate flower bloom, and every leaf that falls in autumn, narrates a tale of continuous transformation, reflecting the ever-evolving character of life itself.

Animals, too, contribute their unique melodies to this symphony, each species playing its part in maintaining balance. The humble bee, in its quest for nectar, facilitates the pollination of plants, driving the cycle of growth, death, and rebirth. Birds spread seeds across vast distances, ensuring the continuation of plant life, while predators regulate the populations of other species, maintaining the delicate balance of ecosystems.

In nature, there is a deep understanding of coexistence, a mutual give-and-take that ensures the survival of all. The elements, too, play their parts—earth, air, fire, and water, each lending its strength, each influencing the unfolding of life.

Despite nature's wisdom and resilience, it is not immune to harm. Human activity has often upset this balance, leading to loss of biodiversity, climate change, and environmental degradation. Recognizing and respecting nature's intricate symphony is critical to our survival, not only as individual species but as a part of this interconnected orchestra.

Nature teaches us about harmony, resilience, interdependence, and the vital importance of preserving balance. It humbles us with its grandeur, inspires us with its beauty, and enlightens us with its wisdom. To listen to nature, to truly appreciate its melody, is to understand our place within this magnificent symphony of life.

Conflict and Resolution

Conflict is an intrinsic part of the human experience, arising from differences in needs, values, goals, or perceptions. It can occur on an interpersonal level, within groups, or between nations, and can take many forms, from minor disagreements to major disputes or wars. While often viewed negatively, conflict, when approached constructively, can also lead to growth, change, and deeper understanding.

Conflict arises from a variety of sources. It can stem from differences in beliefs, interests, or values, or from perceived threats to one's needs or identity. It can be driven by scarcity of resources, competition, power imbalances, or communication breakdowns.

In its most destructive form, conflict can lead to hostility, violence, suffering, and division. It can cause harm, breed resentment, and create cycles of retaliation. However, it's important to recognize that conflict itself is not inherently negative. It's how we handle conflict that determines its impact on our lives and relationships.

At its best, conflict can be a catalyst for positive change. It can bring underlying issues to light, promote dialogue and understanding, and foster creativity and innovation. It can challenge the status quo, inspire new ideas, and drive progress. It can also strengthen relationships by fostering empathy, promoting mutual understanding, and facilitating compromise and resolution.

Managing conflict effectively requires a variety of skills and strategies. These may include active listening, effective communication, empathy, negotiation, and problem-solving. It involves recognizing and validating each other's needs and perspectives, seeking common ground, and striving for mutually satisfactory outcomes.

One key aspect of conflict resolution is the shift from a win-lose mindset to a win-win mindset. This means moving away from viewing conflict as a competition where one side wins at the expense of the other, towards seeing it as a cooperative endeavor where both sides can gain and learn.

Another key aspect is the ability to separate the person from the problem. This involves focusing on the issue at hand rather than blaming or attacking the individual, and recognizing that people's actions and viewpoints are often influenced by a complex array of factors.

Ultimately, conflict is not something to be avoided, but to be navigated with understanding, skill, and compassion. By viewing conflict as an opportunity for growth and transformation, we can turn challenges into stepping stones towards greater understanding, collaboration, and harmony.

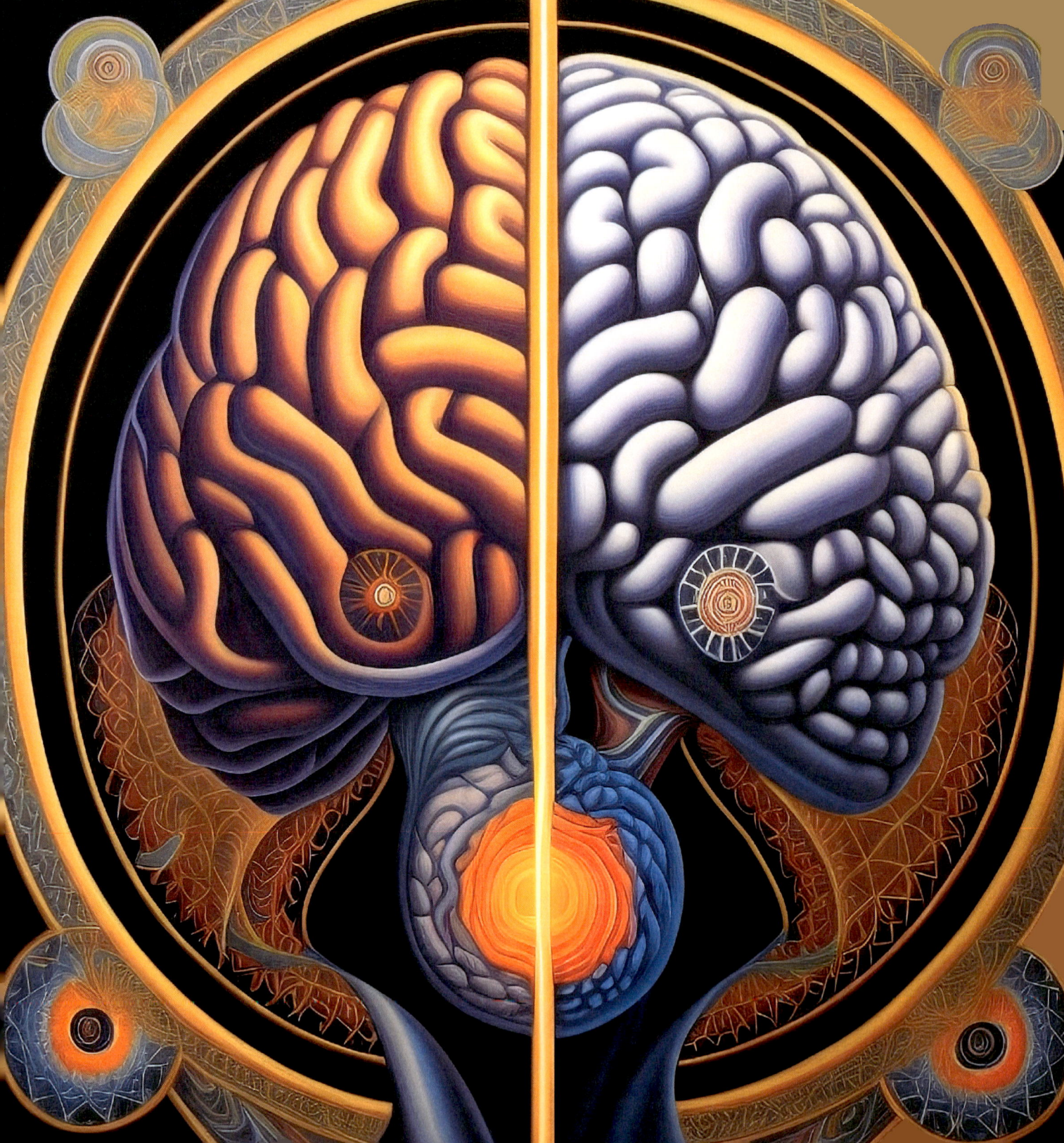

Mystery and Enigma of Dreams

Dreams, in their myriad forms, are an intrinsic part of the human experience. They serve as a bridge between our conscious and unconscious realms, offering glimpses into the depth and breadth of our inner worlds. Dreams can be seen as nightly journeys into our subconscious, laden with symbolism, emotion, and potential insight.

In a literal sense, dreams occur during the Rapid Eye Movement (REM) stage of sleep. During this time, our brain activity is high, resembling that of being awake. The content of our dreams can range from the mundane to the bizarre, often reflecting fragments of our daily experiences, thoughts, and emotions. Yet, the exact purpose of dreams is still a topic of ongoing scientific debate. Some theories propose that dreaming could play roles in memory consolidation, problem-solving, or emotional regulation.

On a psychological level, dreams have been a subject of fascination and interpretation throughout human history. In many cultures, dreams have been seen as prophetic or divine messages. Sigmund Freud, the founder of psychoanalysis, saw dreams as the "royal road to the unconscious," embodying our repressed desires and unresolved conflicts. Carl Jung, another pioneer of psychology, viewed dreams as a means of psychological integration, mirroring our process of individuation and personal growth.

In a metaphorical sense, dreams also represent our aspirations, goals, and visions for the future. They embody what we yearn for, what we strive towards, and what we hope to become. These dreams can serve as a compass, guiding us towards our desired destination in life.

Whether literal or metaphorical, dreams invite us to explore beyond the surface of our conscious minds. They encourage us to delve into the depths of our subconscious, to confront our fears, to understand our desires, and to unearth our hidden potentials. They challenge us to decode their symbolism, to uncover their wisdom, and to glean insights from their narratives.

Dreams, in all their mystery and enigma, are a testament to the complexity and richness of our inner lives. They offer a window into our subconscious, a mirror reflecting our inner selves, and a canvas upon which our imagination and emotions can freely express. By paying attention to our dreams, we can deepen our self-awareness, enhance our personal growth, and enrich our understanding of the human experience.

Change and Transistion

Change is the very fabric of life, a constant flux that permeates every level of our existence. It shapes our world, our societies, and our individual lives. From the ceaseless cycle of seasons to the relentless tide of evolution, change is an inherent part of the cosmos.

Change can be subtle or dramatic, gradual or sudden. It can be born out of necessity, spurred by innovation, or driven by the natural progression of time. It can manifest in our personal lives as shifts in circumstances, relationships, or self-perception. On a broader scale, change is reflected in social trends, technological advances, and shifts in cultural or political landscapes.

Change can be both exhilarating and daunting. It can bring about growth, renewal, and opportunities, yet it can also pose challenges, induce uncertainty, or cause loss. It can be a catalyst for progress, yet it can also engender resistance or fear. The way we perceive and respond to change often depends on our mindset, our resilience, and our capacity to adapt.

Resistance to change is a natural human tendency, often stemming from fear of the unknown, comfort in familiarity, or perceived threat to status or security. However, resisting change is akin to resisting the flow of life. It can lead to stagnation, missed opportunities, or inability to cope with evolving circumstances.

Embracing change, on the other hand, involves accepting the impermanence of life, cultivating adaptability, and viewing change as an opportunity for growth and learning. It involves recognizing that change is not inherently good or bad, but simply a fact of life.

Adapting to change requires flexibility, resilience, and openness. It involves letting go of rigid expectations, adjusting our sails in response to the winds of change, and cultivating a growth mindset. It also involves learning from our experiences, turning challenges into stepping stones, and seizing opportunities for innovation and improvement.

In a world that is constantly changing, the ability to adapt and grow with change is a key aspect of resilience and survival.

Forgiveness

Forgiveness is a profound act of releasing resentment or vengeance towards oneself or another who has caused harm or wrongdoing. It is a process that promotes healing and the restoration of peace, often serving as a pivotal step in reconciliation and the mending of relationships.

It's important to understand that forgiveness is not about denying or minimizing the hurt caused. Nor does it necessarily mean forgetting or condoning the wrongdoing. Rather, forgiveness is about choosing to let go of the hold that the hurt has on you. It's about liberating oneself from the burdens of anger, bitterness, and resentment, and making space for healing, compassion, and peace.

The act of forgiveness can often be challenging, particularly when the pain or betrayal is deep. It may require time, patience, and a willingness to confront and process difficult emotions. At times, it may also require assistance, such as through counseling or mediation.

Forgiveness is not solely for the benefit of the offender but perhaps even more so for the one who has been wronged. Holding onto resentment can be likened to carrying a heavy weight—it exhausts and impedes us, often causing more harm to ourselves than to the person who caused the initial hurt. On the other hand, forgiving can lead to numerous benefits, including reduced stress and anxiety, lower blood pressure, improved mental health, and increased empathy and understanding.

Forgiving oneself is also a crucial aspect of forgiveness. We all make mistakes, and harboring guilt or self-blame can be destructive. Self-forgiveness involves acknowledging our errors, learning from them, making amends where possible, and then choosing to release self-condemnation. This is an integral part of self-compassion and personal growth.

Forgiveness also plays a key role in societal contexts, contributing to conflict resolution, reconciliation, and peace-building. History is replete with inspiring examples of forgiveness, even in the face of horrific atrocities, that have paved the way for healing and reconciliation.

Forgiveness is a gift we give to ourselves. It is a liberating act that frees us from the chains of the past and opens the door to a future of greater peace, compassion, and inner freedom. It is a testament to the strength and resilience of the human spirit, and a beacon of hope for a more compassionate and peaceful world.

Confronting Reality with Hope

Hope is a powerful force, a beacon of light in the dark, a lifeline in tumultuous times. It's an optimistic state of mind that is based on the expectation of positive outcomes. In essence, hope is the belief in possibilities, the conviction that better days lie ahead, and the resilience to strive towards them.

Hope is not merely wishful thinking or blind optimism. It is a dynamic, active process that involves setting goals, devising strategies, and motivating oneself to achieve them. It is a driving force that propels us forward, fuels our ambition, and shapes our vision for the future.

Hope plays a crucial role in our lives, shaping how we navigate challenges and uncertainties. It's like an anchor that keeps us grounded in times of storm, a compass that guides us towards our aspirations, and a spark that ignites our willpower and determination.

In the face of adversity, hope provides the resilience to endure, the strength to persevere, and the courage to forge ahead. It encourages us to view obstacles not as insurmountable barriers but as stepping stones towards our goals. It helps us to transform challenges into opportunities, setbacks into comebacks, and failures into lessons.

Hope has a profound impact on our well-being. Research has shown that hope is associated with numerous benefits, including reduced stress, enhanced resilience, improved mental health, and increased life satisfaction. Hope has also been linked to better physical health outcomes, including improved immune function, reduced disease progression, and increased longevity.

Hope should not be mistaken for an escapist fantasy or a passive waiting. It is not about denying reality or evading responsibility. Instead, it's about confronting the reality with courage, embracing the possibilities with conviction, and shaping the future with diligence.

Hope is also a collective phenomenon. It is something we share, something we inspire in others, and something we build together. It reminds us of our interconnectedness, our shared aspirations, and our collective capacity to create a better world.

Hope is an integral part of the human experience, a fundamental aspect of our survival, and a catalyst for our growth and transformation. It is a testament to our resilience, our adaptability, and our ceaseless striving for betterment.

Humility

Humility is a virtue that is often misunderstood, yet it holds immeasurable value in our interactions with ourselves and the world around us. It is not about self-deprecation or a lack of self-esteem, rather, humility is a balanced, accurate understanding of oneself and a respectful appreciation of others.

Humility is the recognition of our inherent interdependence. It is understanding that we are part of a larger whole and that each of us has something valuable to offer. It is acknowledging our own strengths and accomplishments, while also being aware of our weaknesses and limitations.

Humility involves seeing and accepting ourselves as we truly are, without pretense or illusion. It means being open to learning and growth, admitting when we are wrong, and being willing to change our perspectives or behaviors when necessary. A humble person does not need to prove their worth or superiority but instead finds value in their authenticity and in the cultivation of understanding and compassion.

Humility enables us to appreciate the value and worth of others. It allows us to listen deeply, to learn from different perspectives, and to engage with others in a way that honors their inherent dignity and worth. It encourages cooperation, fosters respect, and builds stronger, more harmonious relationships.

In a world often driven by ego, status, and power, humility is a refreshing and potent counterforce. It keeps us grounded and centered, reminding us of our shared humanity and the broader context in which our lives unfold. It promotes empathy, fairness, and social harmony, thereby contributing to a more compassionate and inclusive society.

Humility enhances our capacity for learning and personal growth. By maintaining an open mind, recognizing our knowledge gaps, and welcoming new insights and experiences, we cultivate a lifelong learning mindset. As the ancient philosopher Socrates wisely stated, "I know that I am intelligent, because I know that I know nothing."

Humility is about embracing the full spectrum of our human experience with honesty, openness, and respect. It is about recognizing and honoring the inherent value within each of us and fostering a spirit of shared learning, mutual respect, and collective progress. Humility, in its truest form, is a profound expression of wisdom, strength, and love.

Power of Gratitude

Gratitude is the recognition and appreciation of the good in our lives, a heartful acknowledgment of the kindness, beauty, and abundance that surround us. It is a perspective that focuses on what we have rather than what we lack, encouraging us to cherish our blessings and to reciprocate kindness and generosity.

Being truly grateful is a profound act of awareness. It is about noticing the simple pleasures, the acts of kindness, the beauty in nature, the joy in relationships, and the multitude of gifts that each day presents us. It is about taking a moment to pause, to savor, to appreciate, and to express our thanks.

Gratitude has a transformative power. It can turn a meal into a feast, a house into a home, a stranger into a friend. It can turn routine jobs into joy, and change ordinary opportunities into blessings. It can fill our hearts with joy, our minds with positivity, and our lives with fulfillment.

Gratitude has numerous psychological and physical benefits. Studies have shown that practicing gratitude can enhance well-being, reduce stress, improve relationships, and foster resilience. It can boost our mood, improve our sleep, enhance our physical health, and even increase our lifespan.

Perhaps the most profound effect of gratitude is its capacity to foster happiness. Happiness does not necessarily make us grateful, but gratitude surely makes us happy. By shifting our focus from what's wrong to what's right, from what we lack to what we have, from the negatives to the positives, gratitude nurtures an enduring sense of happiness and contentment.

Gratitude also has a social dimension. It connects us to others, strengthens our relationships, and fosters a sense of community. It encourages us to express our appreciation, to return kindness, and to pay it forward, thereby promoting a cycle of positivity, generosity, and mutual support.

Cultivating gratitude requires conscious effort. It involves making time to count our blessings, to savor the good in our lives, and to express our appreciation. It may involve keeping a gratitude journal, writing thank-you notes, or simply taking a moment each day to reflect on what we're grateful for.

Gratitude is a powerful and enriching practice that can transform our lives. It is a perspective that magnifies the good, a virtue that enriches the soul, and a habit that nurtures happiness.

Bedrock of Equality

Equality is the bedrock principle upon which fair and just societies are built. It stands for the belief that all individuals, irrespective of their race, gender, age, religion, disability, sexual orientation, or any other status, should be treated with the same dignity and respect, and should have equal rights, freedoms, and opportunities.

Equality is about recognizing and affirming the inherent worth and dignity of every individual. It is about ensuring that every person has an equal chance to make the most of their lives and talents, and that no person should have poorer life chances because of where, what, or to whom they were born.

Equality, however, does not mean uniformity or sameness. It is not about treating everyone exactly the same way, but rather about ensuring that everyone has what they need to enjoy their rights fully. This often requires recognizing and accommodating differences and taking positive measures to redress existing disadvantages.

Equality is crucial not only for individuals but also for societies at large. It fosters social cohesion, promotes mutual respect and understanding, and contributes to peace and stability. Inequalities, on the other hand, can lead to conflict, social fragmentation, and can hinder economic and social development.

Equality is a fundamental human right, enshrined in international human rights law. It requires that all individuals are treated equally under the law and are granted equal protection and benefit of the law. It also prohibits discrimination on any ground and obliges states to take measures to promote equality.

Promoting equality, however, requires more than legal measures. It requires societal change. It involves challenging stereotypes, prejudices, and harmful social norms. It requires promoting diversity and inclusion, empowering marginalized groups, and fostering a culture of respect and mutual understanding.

Equality is also closely linked to other principles such as justice, fairness, and equity. While equality focuses on ensuring that everyone is treated the same way, equity emphasizes the need to take into account the different situations of individuals and to adjust treatment accordingly to achieve a fair outcome.

Equality is a fundamental and universal principle that affirms the inherent dignity and worth of every individual. It is a cornerstone of human rights and social justice, and an indispensable requirement for the achievement of a fair, inclusive, and peaceful society.

Multifaceted Aspects of Justice

Justice is a fundamental moral and ethical principle that signifies fairness, equality, and respect for dignity, human rights, and the rule of law. It serves as the foundation for the harmonious functioning of any society, setting the guidelines for interpersonal behavior, societal order, and institutional operations.

Justice is about fairness. It is the concept that actions should have appropriate consequences, and individuals should be rewarded or punished based on their actions' merits. In the social sphere, justice ensures the fair distribution of resources, opportunities, and privileges, and it protects against any form of discrimination or bias.

Justice also embodies respect for human rights, ensuring that all individuals' inherent rights are acknowledged and protected. It advocates for the preservation of personal freedoms and equality, defending the dignity of every individual regardless of their background, belief, or status.

In terms of the rule of law, justice is reflected in the fair, unbiased application and execution of laws. It is vital for maintaining societal order, providing a framework for resolving disputes, and defining the boundaries of acceptable conduct. The principles of legal justice require that laws be clear, public, fair, and applied equally to all members of society. Justice is served when punishment meets the crime, and when the innocent are protected.

Pursuing justice isn't merely a societal or institutional endeavor, but also a personal one. It involves cultivating a sense of fairness, standing up against prejudice and discrimination, and advocating for those who may be marginalized or disempowered.

Justice plays a pivotal role in creating a society that promotes peace, harmony, and cooperation. It encourages a sense of trust among individuals, leading to more collaborative and mutually respectful relationships. A just society allows for social cohesion and provides the grounds for human advancement.

Yet, the pursuit of justice is a continuous journey. It requires constant vigilance, courage, and commitment to challenge injustice, correct imbalances, and strive for a fair and equitable world.

Justice is a multifaceted principle that stands as a pillar of society, contributing to the maintenance of order, protection of rights, and the promotion of societal cohesion. It is a dynamic concept, ever-evolving to meet the demands of a changing world, forever committed to its core tenets of fairness, respect for dignity, and the rule of law.

Complexities of Truth

Truth is a fundamental cornerstone of our shared reality, a beacon that guides our understanding of the world and our interactions within it. It is the compass by which we navigate our perceptions, beliefs, decisions, and actions.

Truth, in its essence, is a congruence between perception and reality. It is when what we believe or say aligns with the actual state of affairs. It's the bedrock upon which knowledge and wisdom are built, serving as the key to authentic communication, understanding, and growth.

The pursuit of truth is a journey of exploration and discovery. It involves an ongoing process of questioning, learning, testing, and refining our understanding. It requires an open mind, a sense of curiosity, and a commitment to evidence and reason.

Truth also carries a moral dimension. It calls for honesty, integrity, and transparency in our thoughts, words, and actions. To be truthful means to be genuine, to live authentically, and to communicate sincerely. It involves standing by one's convictions, admitting one's mistakes, and striving for consistency between one's values, words, and actions.

Truth is not always clear-cut or easy to discern. It can often be complex, multi-faceted, and nuanced. It can be obscured by biases, misconceptions, or false information. Therefore, the pursuit of truth requires critical thinking, discernment, and vigilance. It demands that we challenge assumptions, scrutinize sources, consider multiple perspectives, and remain open to new information or revisions of understanding.

Truth is vital to the health and functioning of society. It forms the basis of trust, credibility, and accountability. It is essential for informed decision-making, effective communication, and constructive dialogue. It is a bulwark against manipulation, deceit, and corruption.

In a broader philosophical or spiritual context, truth is often associated with the ultimate reality or the fundamental nature of existence. It represents the quest for deeper understanding, self-realization, and spiritual enlightenment.

Truth is a cornerstone of personal integrity and societal health. It is an ongoing pursuit, a moral duty, and a guiding light. It invites us to live authentically, to think critically, and to engage with the world with openness, curiosity, and discernment.

Transformative Faith

Faith is a profound and personal belief that often transcends the bounds of rational explanation. It's a confidence or trust in something or someone, often without concrete proof or empirical evidence. It can provide a sense of purpose, offer a moral compass, bring comfort during trials, and even inspire actions towards a greater good.

Faith often finds its most recognized expression in religious contexts, where it denotes a firm belief in divine entities, teachings, or spiritual realities. Yet, faith extends beyond religious dimensions. It is an inherent part of the human condition, permeating our relationships, aspirations, pursuits, and perceptions of the world.

In interpersonal relationships, faith manifests as trust. It is the trust we place in people's words, promises, or actions. It is the invisible bond that connects individuals, fosters cooperation, and forms the foundation of strong relationships and communities.

In our personal journeys, faith is the inner assurance that propels us towards our goals, even in the face of uncertainties and setbacks. It is the belief in our potential, the conviction of our values, and the hope for a better future. This kind of faith is a powerful motivator, pushing us to strive, persevere, and actualize our dreams.

In the quest for knowledge and truth, faith is the willingness to accept certain truths while we continue to explore and seek understanding. It's the acceptance that some aspects of reality may currently lie beyond our comprehension, yet we have the confidence that with time, patience, and effort, we may eventually unravel them.

Faith and reason are not mutually exclusive. A balanced perspective appreciates the role of empirical evidence and logical reasoning, while also recognizing the value and necessity of faith in areas where certainty may not be attainable.

Faith also has transformative potential. It can foster resilience in the face of adversity, inspire acts of kindness and compassion, and contribute to a sense of peace and contentment.

Faith is often shaped and refined through personal experiences, reflections, doubts, and realizations. It is not a static state but a dynamic and evolving process.

Faith is a multifaceted and deeply personal aspect of human experience. It is a powerful force that can provide a sense of purpose, guide our actions, deepen our relationships, and inspire our pursuit of knowledge and truth.

Human Suffering

Suffering is an intrinsic part of the human condition. It comes in many forms, be it physical pain, emotional distress, loss, or existential angst. It's a universal experience that transcends cultures, histories, and individual identities.

Suffering often arises from circumstances beyond our control—illness, accidents, natural disasters, or the actions of others. It can also stem from our own thoughts, emotions, and actions, such as when we are gripped by guilt, regret, fear, or self-doubt. Suffering is not always visible; it can be a deeply private experience, tucked away beneath the surface of our daily lives.

While suffering is undeniably painful and challenging, it also has the potential to be a catalyst for growth, transformation, and deeper understanding. It can strip away superficial concerns and distractions, pushing us to confront fundamental aspects of our existence. In the face of suffering, we are often compelled to question, reflect, and seek meaning and purpose in our lives.

Suffering can deepen our compassion, empathy, and interconnectedness. As we become aware of our own suffering and the imperfection of life, we may become more attuned to the suffering of others. This understanding can kindle a sense of shared humanity, leading to acts of kindness, solidarity, and support.

Learning to cope with suffering is a critical part of our journey. Different people have different ways of navigating suffering. Some may find solace and strength in their faith, spiritual practices, or philosophical beliefs. Others may draw upon the support of loved ones, the help of professionals, or the healing power of creative expression.

Many philosophical and spiritual traditions regard the understanding and transcendence of suffering as a central part of human growth. For instance, in Buddhism, the Four Noble Truths delineate the nature of suffering, its origin, its cessation, and the path leading to its cessation, serving as a guide towards liberation and enlightenment.

Recognizing that while suffering is a part of life, unnecessary or preventable suffering—caused by violence, injustice, inequality, or neglect—must be actively addressed and alleviated by societal action and systemic changes.

Suffering, while an undeniably difficult aspect of human existence, carries within it the seeds of growth, compassion, and understanding. It underscores our shared vulnerability and the profound need for kindness, support, and connection.

Mindfulness

Mindfulness is the practice of focusing our attention on the present moment in a purposeful and non-judgmental way. It's about being fully engaged and present in whatever we are doing or experiencing at any given time, rather than being lost in thoughts, concerns, or distractions.

Mindfulness allows us to experience life more directly, rather than through the lens of past memories or future expectations. It invites us to see, hear, and feel the world around us as it is, rather than how we think it should be. It's about noticing the details, the nuances, the changes, and the constants.

When we practice mindfulness, we learn to pay attention to our thoughts and emotions without getting caught up in them. We learn to observe them as they come and go, without judging them or identifying with them. This gives us a deeper understanding of our mental processes and can help us manage our emotions more effectively.

Mindfulness also involves cultivating an attitude of acceptance and kindness towards ourselves. Rather than being critical or harsh, we learn to treat ourselves with the same patience, understanding, and compassion that we would extend to a good friend.

Practicing mindfulness can bring numerous benefits, reducing stress, anxiety, and depression. It can improve our focus, creativity, and cognitive abilities. It can enhance our relationships, improve our health, and increase our overall wellbeing.

Mindfulness can be practiced in many ways. Formal mindfulness practices include meditation techniques such as sitting meditation, walking meditation, or body scan meditation. Informal practices involve bringing mindful awareness to everyday activities such as eating, washing dishes, or simply breathing.

In a broader context, mindfulness encourages us to live more consciously and deliberately. It invites us to pause, to reflect, and to engage fully with life. It helps us to cultivate an inner peace that is not dependent on external circumstances, but rather on our own awareness and understanding.

Mindfulness is a powerful practice that can enrich our lives in numerous ways. It is a path to greater self-awareness, emotional balance, and a deeper appreciation of life's simple moments.

Powers of Perception

Perception is the window through which we experience our world. It's our personal lens, coloring, shaping, and making sense of the reality around us. It's not just about what we see, hear, touch, taste, or smell—it's about how we interpret these experiences, how we weave them into our understanding of existence.

Every perception begins as a simple sensory input, yet no perception ends there. Our minds take these raw stimuli and filter them through our past experiences, beliefs, values, biases, and emotions, transforming them into our subjective experiences. Thus, our perception of reality is intrinsically linked to who we are, embodying our unique blend of experiences and perspectives.

Two people can stand in the same place, at the same time, looking at the same scene, yet perceive it entirely differently. One may see beauty and harmony, the other chaos and discord. One might find calm, the other anxiety. Perception is what turns a melody into music or noise, a sunset into a spectacle of colors or a sign of impending darkness.

Perception also plays a crucial role in our interactions with others. How we perceive others influences our reactions towards them, and in turn, shapes their responses towards us. By consciously choosing empathy and understanding, we can adjust our perceptions and foster healthier, more compassionate interactions.

The power of perception extends to our self-view as well. It influences our self-esteem, our sense of purpose, our capacity for joy. Recognizing this, we can seek to cultivate a perception of ourselves that emphasizes our potential, our growth, our inherent worthiness.

Perception, in essence, is our personalized map of reality. It's an ever-evolving work in progress that we can influence and shape. Through introspection, mindfulness, and an openness to new experiences, we can expand our perceptions, invite in greater understanding, and navigate our lives with deeper awareness and insight. In this way, our perception becomes more than just a passive receptacle of experience—it becomes an active tool for personal growth and transformation.

Cultivating Creativity

Creativity, in essence, is the ability to perceive connections, possibilities, and patterns that others might overlook, and then to combine these elements in new and meaningful ways. It is the birthplace of innovation, the wellspring of art, and a vital component of problem-solving. While we often associate creativity with artists, musicians, or writers, it is, in fact, a universal human trait that can be cultivated and enriched.

The first step in cultivating creativity is to create space for it. Creativity often emerges in moments of quiet reflection and solitude. Dedicating time to simply sit with your thoughts, daydream, or engage in free writing can open the door to creative insights.

Curiosity and open-mindedness are two of the most powerful fuels for creativity. By questioning the status quo, exploring different perspectives, and pushing the boundaries of your own knowledge, you ignite the creative spark. Read widely, travel, learn new skills, ask questions, and keep an open mind. Remember that no field or subject is irrelevant. The more diverse your experiences and knowledge, the richer your creative well.

Creative thinking is often characterized by the ability to perceive connections between seemingly unrelated concepts. This can be practiced. Challenge yourself to find links between diverse ideas or to approach problems from completely new angles. Metaphorical thinking can be especially powerful in this regard.

Creativity thrives in environments that encourage risk-taking and value originality. Don't be afraid to make mistakes or to share your out-of-the-box ideas. Remember that many of the world's most creative minds faced rejection and criticism. Persist in the face of setbacks and keep pushing the boundaries of your imagination.

Understand that creativity is a process, not an event. Ideas often need time to incubate. If you're feeling stuck, step away from your project for a bit. Engage in activities that relax and energize you. Physical movement, nature walks, or even mundane chores can provide unexpected creative breakthroughs.

Trust in your unique creative process, be patient with yourself, and enjoy the journey of discovery that creativity brings. Above all, remember that everyone possesses the capacity for creativity. It's not a rare gift reserved for a select few, but a natural part of the human experience that we can all tap into and cultivate.

Power Dynamics

Power dynamics pervade every aspect of human interaction - from interpersonal relationships, to workplaces, to politics on a global scale. Understanding them is critical to navigating and interpreting the world around us.

Power is the ability to influence others and control resources. It can be formal, derived from a specific role or position, or informal, stemming from knowledge, charisma, or relationships. The dynamics of power revolve around who has it, how it's used, and how it affects those involved.

In interpersonal relationships, power dynamics are often shaped by factors such as wealth, physical strength, intelligence, and social status. These dynamics can influence everything from decision-making to conflict resolution. A balanced power dynamic is crucial for healthy relationships. Imbalances can lead to manipulation, control, and abuse. Open communication, respect, and mutual understanding can help mitigate these imbalances.

In the workplace, power dynamics can shape career trajectories, organizational culture, and productivity. Managers and leaders wield power over their subordinates, but power also flows from the bottom up, as employees can influence their superiors through feedback, collective bargaining, and personal influence.

In society at large, power dynamics are shaped by factors such as gender, race, age, economic status, and education. These dynamics often determine who gets heard, who gets to make decisions, and who benefits from societal resources and opportunities.

Power dynamics play a significant role in global politics. Nations exercise power through economic strength, military might, diplomatic influence, and cultural appeal. The balance of power among nations shapes international relations, affecting everything from trade agreements to conflict resolution.

Understanding power dynamics requires introspection and empathy. It requires us to examine our own power and privilege, and how these may affect others. By doing so, we can strive for more equitable power dynamics that uphold the dignity and worth of all individuals.

Power dynamics shape our interactions and our society at large. Recognizing them allows us to better understand the world around us and to act in ways that promote fairness, respect, and mutual benefit.

Energy. Prana. Reiki. Qi.

Energy is a fundamental concept that underpins our understanding of the physical universe and our experience of life. It manifests in various forms, and its constant transformation from one form to another drives the processes and changes we observe in the world around us.

In physics, energy is defined as the capacity to do work. It can be stored in various forms, such as potential energy, kinetic energy, thermal energy, chemical energy, and nuclear energy, to name a few. The law of conservation of energy, one of the basic laws of physics, states that energy cannot be created or destroyed, only transferred or converted from one form to another.

But energy is not just a physical phenomenon. It also permeates our subjective experiences and everyday lives in less tangible but equally significant ways. We often use the term 'energy' to describe our vitality, mood, or emotional state. We speak of 'high energy' or 'low energy' days, 'positive' or 'negative' energy in people or environments, and the 'flow' of energy in our bodies and minds.

In many spiritual and philosophical traditions, energy is viewed as the vital life force that animates all living beings and connects them with each other and the universe. In traditional Chinese culture, this energy is called 'Qi'; in Indian traditions, it's known as 'Prana'. The practice of energy healing, such as Reiki, and the concept of Chakras or energy centers in the body, stem from this understanding of energy.

Energy is also a key concept in environmental and sustainability discussions. The way we produce and consume energy has significant implications for our planet's health and our collective future. Renewable energy sources like wind, solar, and hydropower offer sustainable alternatives to fossil fuels, reducing our carbon footprint and helping mitigate climate change.

In our personal lives, understanding and managing our energy is crucial for maintaining our physical, mental, and emotional health. Regular exercise, adequate sleep, a balanced diet, stress management, and mindfulness practices can all contribute to better energy levels and overall well-being.

Energy is a universal principle that operates on multiple levels, from the cosmic and environmental scales down to our personal experiences and inner states. Understanding the nature and dynamics of energy can enhance our understanding of the world, our relationships with others, and our own selves, promoting a more balanced, vibrant, and sustainable life.

Navigating Pride

Pride is a complex emotion and trait, carrying both positive and negative connotations, depending on its source and expression.

On one hand, pride can serve as a mark of self-esteem and self-respect. It can be an acknowledgment of one's own worth and accomplishments, a sense of satisfaction and fulfilment derived from one's efforts, achievements, or abilities. This form of pride is often linked to resilience, perseverance, and the motivation to strive for excellence. It reflects a positive self-regard and can be a driving force for personal growth and constructive action.

On the other hand, pride can also take on a more problematic form when it becomes excessive or misplaced, transforming into arrogance or hubris. This happens when one starts to believe oneself to be inherently superior to others, disregarding their views, feelings, or rights. This kind of pride can lead to an inflated ego, a sense of entitlement, and a lack of empathy or understanding for others.

Pride can sometimes turn into a defensive mechanism that prevents individuals from admitting their mistakes or shortcomings, hindering personal growth and fostering unhealthy relationships. In many wisdom traditions, such as those found in various spiritual and philosophical teachings, this type of pride is often identified as a major barrier to self-awareness and spiritual growth.

In a societal context, pride can also be collective. This is seen in the pride we feel as members of a community, nation, or group, derived from shared achievements, traditions, or values. Like individual pride, collective pride can both unite and divide, fostering a sense of belonging and identity, but also potentially leading to exclusion, prejudice, or aggression towards those outside the group.

Navigating pride requires self-awareness, balance, and a grounded sense of self-worth. It involves cultivating a sense of pride that acknowledges our achievements and boosts our self-esteem, without losing sight of our interconnectedness and shared humanity. It's about appreciating our unique strengths and qualities, while also recognizing that every individual has their own set of strengths and qualities that are equally worthy of respect.

Pride is a double-edged sword that can either contribute to our growth and well-being or become a stumbling block in our relationships and personal development. The key lies in balancing a healthy sense of self-worth with humility and respect for others, transforming pride from a potential vice into a source of motivation, resilience, and positive self-regard.

Enriching Generosity

Generosity is a virtue that speaks volumes about the human spirit. It is an intentional act of kindness, driven by the heartfelt desire to improve the lives of others without expecting anything in return. It is a quality that transcends material wealth, for one can be generous with time, with kindness, with knowledge, and even with simple acts of compassion.

True generosity is not measured by the size of a gift, but by the spirit in which it is given. A small act offered with genuine love can have a profound impact. Giving isn't merely transactional—it's transformational. It has the power to change the lives of both the giver and the receiver.

Generosity teaches us about empathy and compassion. By putting ourselves in the shoes of others, we come to understand their struggles and their needs. This deepens our connection to our fellow human beings, fostering a sense of community and mutual support.

Yet, generosity is not merely about giving away material possessions. It extends to the way we treat others. Being generous with our time, with our patience, with our understanding, and with our forgiveness can often mean more than any physical gift.

One remarkable aspect of generosity is its potential to create a ripple effect. A single act of generosity can inspire others to act in kind, setting off a chain of positivity and kindness. This is often referred to as "paying it forward."

But there's a balance to be struck, for true generosity should not leave one depleted or taken advantage of. It requires discernment, ensuring that our acts of giving genuinely serve others and do not foster dependency or harm.

Generosity also brings with it a profound sense of fulfillment. Studies have consistently shown that generous individuals often lead happier, more fulfilled lives. In giving, we receive—a truth that speaks to the interconnected nature of human beings.

Generosity is more than an act—it is a way of life, a path that leads us towards empathy, connection, and ultimately, our shared humanity. By cultivating generosity in our daily lives, we can bring about positive change in ourselves, in our relationships, and in our communities.

Empathy

Empathy, the capacity to understand and share the feelings of others, is a profound human ability that connects us all. It is the conduit through which we can bridge our own experiences with those of others, fostering a sense of common understanding and shared humanity.

Empathy goes a step further than sympathy, which is feeling compassion for others in their times of distress – it is feeling with others, entering their world and connecting with their emotions on a deeper level. It allows us to perceive and share another person's innermost feelings, not as a distant observer, but as if they are our own.

Being empathetic begins with active listening. This involves not just hearing the words that another person is saying but paying attention to the emotions behind those words and responding to them in a thoughtful and compassionate way. It involves acknowledging their feelings, showing them that they are seen and heard, and that their emotions are valid.

Empathy also involves perspective-taking. It requires us to put aside our own worldview for a moment and try to see things from another's point of view. This can be challenging, especially when their experiences or beliefs differ from ours, but it's a crucial part of building understanding and connection.

Importantly, empathy also means recognizing the common humanity in all of us. Regardless of our differences, we all experience joy, sorrow, fear, and love. When we acknowledge this, it becomes easier to relate to the feelings of others, even when their experiences are different from ours.

Empathy has the power to break down barriers and build bridges. It fosters tolerance, understanding, and unity in a world that can often feel divided. It enables us to respond to each other with kindness, compassion, and decency, reminding us that at our core, we all share the same basic human needs and desires.

Being empathetic doesn't mean that we have to agree with everyone, or that we have to sacrifice our own well-being to care for others. Rather, it means acknowledging and respecting the full range of human emotions in others as well as in ourselves.

Cultivating empathy is a lifelong journey, but one well worth taking. For in understanding others, we come to better understand ourselves, and in connecting deeply with the experiences of others, we find our own lives enriched.

Boundaries

Boundaries are the invisible lines we draw around ourselves to maintain balance and protect our physical, emotional, and mental well-being. They are vital components of our identity and are crucial in promoting respect, both for ourselves and from others.

Boundaries come in many forms. Physical boundaries pertain to personal space and physical touch. Emotional boundaries involve differentiating our emotions from someone else's and taking responsibility for our feelings. Intellectual boundaries refer to respecting others' ideas and thoughts. Time boundaries mean treating our time and others' as valuable.

Setting healthy boundaries allows us to express who we are and what we need. It creates a clear delineation between what is acceptable and what is not. This promotes self-respect, as well as respect for others, fostering more balanced and fulfilling relationships.

Setting boundaries can be challenging. It often involves tough conversations and the potential for conflict. But remember, it is a necessary process for our mental and emotional health. People may initially resist your boundaries, but with assertiveness and consistency, they will learn to understand and respect them.

Respecting boundaries set by others is equally essential. It helps build trust and foster healthier relationships. If we do not honor others' boundaries, we risk invading their personal space, disregarding their feelings, and undermining their autonomy.

One key aspect of setting boundaries is the understanding that "no" is a complete sentence. You have the right to turn down requests or decline invitations without feeling guilty or needing to justify yourself. This can be a tough habit to adopt, especially if you're used to pleasing others, but it is crucial for maintaining your well-being.

Boundaries are not about isolating ourselves but about engaging with others in a way that respects our individual needs and limits. They allow us to love ourselves and others simultaneously without draining our personal resources.

The essence of boundaries lies in recognizing our worth, prioritizing our well-being, and cultivating respectful relationships. They are not just a line drawn in the sand, but a dynamic expression of our self-respect and our respect for others.

Boundaries create these essential spaces, allowing us to stand alone yet be together in a harmonious balance.

Meditation

Meditation is a practice as ancient as the hills, a timeless technique to cultivate inner stillness, awareness, and harmony. It's an exploration of the inner self, a gentle journey into the silence that expands our consciousness and deepens our understanding of life.

Meditation is essentially is the art of focused attention. It's about grounding yourself in the present moment, bringing your mind back from the wanderings of the past and the anxieties of the future. It's about calming the constant chatter in our minds, allowing us to encounter the tranquility beneath the surface of our thoughts.

There are many forms of meditation, each with its own techniques and methods. Mindfulness meditation encourages us to observe our thoughts without judgment, to simply be present with what is. Concentration meditation focuses our mind on a single object, such as our breath or a mantra. Loving-kindness meditation cultivates feelings of compassion and love toward ourselves and others. Despite the differences in approach, all forms of meditation aim to nurture a state of inner peace and heightened awareness.

Meditation does more than just quiet the mind; it cultivates qualities like compassion, patience, and gratitude. It allows us to observe our thoughts and emotions without getting entangled in them, helping us better manage stress, anxiety, and negative emotions. It fosters mindfulness, the ability to live fully in the present moment, enriching our experiences and encouraging a deeper appreciation of life.

Meditating has profound physiological effects. Research shows it can reduce blood pressure, improve sleep, bolster the immune system, and even alter the structure of the brain in ways that promote attention and emotional balance.

It's really helpful to understand that meditation is not about achieving a certain state, or about eliminating thoughts or emotions. It's about cultivating a gentle, nonjudgmental awareness of whatever arises in the present moment. It's about meeting ourselves where we are, with openness and acceptance.

Engaging in a regular meditation practice can be challenging, especially in our fast-paced, always-connected world. Yet, the rewards are immense. Even a few minutes a day can make a significant difference.

Meditation is the journey of acceptance, of standing firmly in the here and now, and of meeting each moment with grace, presence, and awareness.

Authentic Courage

Courage is often perceived as the ability to face danger, fear, or changes, but its essence delves much deeper. It's not just about daring actions or heroic feats; it's about inner strength, resilience, and the determination to persist in the face of adversity.

At its core, courage is about confronting our own vulnerabilities, uncertainties, and doubts. It involves standing up for what we believe is right, even when it's unpopular or challenging. Courage may mean speaking our truth, even when our voice shakes, or admitting our mistakes and taking responsibility for them, even when it's uncomfortable.

Courage is also closely linked to authenticity. It takes courage to be true to ourselves, to acknowledge our limitations and embrace our unique strengths, and to follow our own path, even when it diverges from societal expectations or norms. Authenticity involves daring to live according to our values and desires, rather than trying to fit into predefined molds.

Learning to be courageous is a fundamental aspect of personal growth and self-transformation. It involves stepping out of our comfort zones, challenging our fears, and opening ourselves to new experiences, ideas, and perspectives. It means being willing to take risks and endure failures and rejections, seeing them not as endings but as learning opportunities and stepping stones towards success.

Courage also extends to our interactions with others. It involves showing empathy and kindness to those who are different from us, standing up against injustice and discrimination, and defending those who can't defend themselves. It's about being a voice for the voiceless and a protector for the vulnerable.

Courage is not about being fearless. On the contrary, courage involves acknowledging our fears and choosing to act despite them. It is about learning to manage fear, not eliminate it. As the saying goes, "Courage is not the absence of fear, but the triumph over it."

Courage is a deeply personal and transformative quality that enables us to live authentically, grow continuously, and contribute positively to the world around us. By cultivating courage, we not only enrich our own lives, but also inspire others and make a difference in the world.

Essential Balance

Balance is a vital element in the grand composition of life. It's a state of equilibrium, a harmonious arrangement that brings peace, stability, and productivity. At its core, balance involves equalizing various aspects of life – not an easy task in our fast-paced, ever-changing world, yet essential for our well-being and fulfillment.

In a physical sense, balance is crucial for maintaining our health. It involves balancing our diet to include diverse nutrients, balancing physical activities with rest and recovery, and even the intricate biochemical balance within our bodies that supports life.

Emotionally, balance helps us navigate through the spectrum of our feelings. It allows us to experience joy, sadness, anger, love, fear, and countless other emotions, without letting any single emotion hijack our well-being. Emotional balance is not about ignoring or suppressing emotions, but acknowledging and expressing them in healthy ways.

Balance is also essential in our mental life. It's about balancing our work and personal life, balancing time spent with others and time spent alone, balancing periods of focused productivity with periods of relaxation and play. A balanced mind is not plagued by extreme stress or lethargy, but navigates between the two with resilience and flexibility.

In relationships, balance is about give and take. It involves respecting personal boundaries and fostering mutual understanding. It's about balancing the needs and desires of self with those of others, understanding that healthy relationships thrive when there is a balance of independence and connection.

At a higher level, balance is also about aligning our actions with our values, balancing our immediate needs with our long-term goals, balancing self-improvement with self-acceptance. It's about balancing the material pursuits with spiritual growth, ambition with contentment, and certainty with curiosity.

Balance is dynamic; it's not a static state to be achieved and preserved forever. It requires continuous adjustments, recalibrations, and mindful attention. Achieving balance does not mean equal time or intensity in all areas, but rather harmony that reflects our unique needs, goals, and circumstances at any given moment.

Balance is a deeply personal fundamental principle of a fulfilling, healthy life. Balance is a fundamental principle of a fulfilling, healthy life. It's about harmony among various aspects of life, leading to overall well-being and peace. By cultivating balance, we can navigate life's challenges with grace, enhance our productivity, and savor the beautiful symphony of life.

Enduring Lifes Challenges

Resilience is an inherent and transformative quality that allows us to navigate through life's challenges, recover from setbacks, and grow stronger in the process. It is not about avoiding or being immune to difficulties, but about facing them head-on and bouncing back each time we fall.

Resilience involves the capacity to manage stress, maintain emotional balance, and preserve mental well-being even in the face of adversity. It's about having the flexibility to adapt to change, the courage to confront our fears, and the determination to persevere through hardships.

At the heart of resilience lies the belief in one's ability to endure and overcome. It is fueled by self-confidence and a sense of self-efficacy. Resilient individuals view challenges as opportunities for learning and growth, rather than as insurmountable obstacles. They see failures not as indicators of personal inadequacy, but as temporary setbacks that provide valuable lessons for future endeavors.

Resilience is fostered by a strong support system. Connections with supportive and caring individuals can provide emotional strength and reassurance during difficult times. Such connections may come from family, friends, mentors, or even broader communities that share similar experiences or objectives.

Resilience also involves practicing self-care and maintaining physical well-being. Regular exercise, a balanced diet, adequate sleep, and mindfulness practices such as meditation can all contribute to our ability to withstand stress and recover from adversities.

Importantly, resilience is not a trait that people either have or do not have. It is not a static or permanent state. Rather, it is a dynamic process that can be learned, cultivated, and strengthened over time. It involves developing coping strategies, building inner resources, fostering supportive relationships, and acquiring new skills and competencies.

Adversities and challenges are inevitable. Yet, it is resilience that enables us to endure these trials, to transform them into stepping stones, and to emerge stronger, wiser, and more compassionate. By cultivating resilience, we can navigate life's storms with grace, turn our wounds into wisdom, and enhance our capacity for joy, fulfillment, and personal growth.

Detachment

Detachment, a concept steeped in wisdom, often misconstrued as indifference, is a conscious and intentional state of being that frees us from unnecessary burdens and allows us to focus on what truly matters. It isn't about distancing oneself from the world, but rather about cultivating a sense of inner peace and clarity that isn't affected by external circumstances. It's about learning to be in the world, fully engaged and present, but not consumed or defined by it.

Cutting the deadwood, a metaphor hailing from the practice of pruning unproductive branches from a tree to promote its growth, parallels the practice of detachment. In the journey of life, we accumulate beliefs, habits, relationships, and pursuits that may no longer serve us, the deadwood of our lives. These are not necessarily harmful in themselves, but they may hinder our growth, cloud our judgment, and divert our resources from what's truly important.

Detachment and cutting the deadwood go hand in hand. The act of cutting the deadwood is a physical manifestation of detachment. It's about acknowledging that holding onto everything—every relationship, every possession, every belief—is not only impractical, but also a barrier to our growth and well-being. It's about letting go of what no longer serves us, making space for the new, the nurturing, and the nourishing.

This process may seem daunting or even painful. The deadwood, despite being unproductive, is familiar and comfortable. Detachment might seem like loss, but in reality, it is about gaining—gaining freedom, clarity, peace, and the potential for new growth.

Detachment, however, is not a call to abandon responsibilities or connections that challenge us. It is about changing our relationship with them. We learn to engage without getting entangled, to love without possessing, to participate without losing ourselves.

In the grand tapestry of life, it's not the quantity of things or people, but the quality of what we hold onto, that shapes our experience. By practicing detachment and cutting the deadwood, we can navigate life with greater grace, make more meaningful contributions, and experience the profound peace that comes from knowing we are not defined by what we hold, but by how we hold it, how we let it go, and how we grow from it.

After Enlightenment

Enlightenment, as explored in various spiritual traditions, signifies a profound understanding of the true nature of existence, a liberation from illusion and ignorance. It's a state of awakening where one experiences a deep connection with all of existence and perceives the inherent interdependence and impermanence of all phenomena.

At the heart of enlightenment lies the realization of 'self' and 'other' as constructs of the mind, a recognition that these dichotomies are a product of our thoughts rather than inherent truths. An enlightened individual perceives beyond these dualities, witnessing a reality where all boundaries dissolve and everything is interconnected.

The journey to enlightenment is not a pursuit of a distant goal or a grand transformation to be achieved. Rather, it's about unveiling the innate wisdom and compassion that are already present within us, beneath layers of conditioning and misconception.

The adage of "Before enlightenment, chop wood, carry water. After enlightenment, chop wood, carry water" beautifully encapsulates the essence of enlightenment. On the surface, it seems to suggest that enlightenment brings no change, that life continues as usual. However, the subtleties lie in the internal transformation and the altered perception of the same activities.

Before enlightenment, one might chop wood and carry water with a mind full of distractions, desires, fears, or judgments. There might be a sense of separateness, a sense of doing these tasks as a means to an end, or with a longing for more fulfilling endeavors.

After enlightenment, while the physical act of chopping wood and carrying water remains the same, the inner experience transforms. These tasks are performed with complete mindfulness, with a deep understanding of their essentiality and their connection to the web of existence. There is no separation between the task, the self, and the universe.

Each chop of the wood and each step to carry the water is no longer seen as mundane work, but as an integral part of the cosmic dance of life. The enlightened mind finds joy and purpose in these simple tasks, recognizing them as expressions of life's interconnectedness and impermanence.

Enlightenment is not about escaping the world or transcending our daily tasks. It is about seeing these tasks and the world itself with new eyes, recognizing the divine in the ordinary, and experiencing oneness in diversity. It's about chopping wood and carrying water with a heart full of joy, a mind full of peace, and a soul connected to the cosmos.

Tapestry of Vibration

Vibration, in its simplest form, is a movement back and forth or an oscillation. It's a fundamental property of the universe itself, a rhythm that permeates every atom, every molecule, every living being, and every system in existence.

From the gentle sway of tree branches in the wind to the steady thump of a heartbeat, from the humming strings of a guitar to the unimaginable vibration of subatomic particles, everything in the universe vibrates. Even the seemingly still earth beneath our feet hums with the vibrational music of geological and atmospheric shifts.

At its heart, vibration is about interaction and energy exchange. Every object and being in the universe maintains a unique vibrational frequency. When two objects or beings come into contact, their vibrations can influence each other. This is known as resonance. A powerful instance of this is when a singer's pitch can cause a glass to shatter. The vibration of the sound waves matches the natural vibration of the glass, causing it to resonate destructively.

In the human realm, we often use the concept of vibration metaphorically. We speak of 'good vibes' or 'bad vibes,' referring to a sense of harmony or dissonance we feel with people, places, or situations. This use of 'vibration' taps into a deep intuitive understanding that our state of being affects and is affected by the states of others around us.

In spiritual and philosophical traditions, vibration is often associated with the life force or energy that animates all beings. Many meditation and mindfulness practices involve tuning into or altering our own vibrational state, often through rhythmic activities like breathing or chanting.

On the grandest scale, the very fabric of our universe – space and time – is understood by physicists to be subject to vibrations. Gravitational waves, ripples in the fabric of spacetime, are essentially vibrations that travel through the universe, caused by the movements of massive objects like black holes and neutron stars.

Vibration is not just a physical phenomenon, but a metaphorical, philosophical, and spiritual principle that captures the dynamic interconnectedness of all things in the universe. Whether we are considering the fluttering of a butterfly's wings, the emotional resonance between people, or the tremors of cosmic bodies, vibration offers a lens to perceive the dance of existence.

Taking Responsibility

Responsibility is a fundamental aspect of our existence that intertwines our relationship with the world around us. It is the acknowledgment and acceptance of the power we possess over our actions, thoughts, and decisions, and the impact they have on our lives and the lives of others.

At its core, responsibility is about choice and accountability. It involves recognizing that we are the architects of our actions and that these actions bear consequences. Each choice we make, each step we take, has a ripple effect, influencing not only our own journey but also touching the lives of others and the world at large.

Embracing responsibility means acknowledging that we are not mere spectators of life, but active participants shaping our destiny. It shifts the focus from blaming external circumstances or individuals for our predicaments to understanding our role in creating or responding to these situations. This shift empowers us to take charge of our lives, to make mindful choices, and to strive towards growth and improvement.

Responsibility also extends beyond the personal sphere. As members of a community, a society, a planet, we have a collective responsibility. This involves caring for each other, respecting diversity, upholding justice, and safeguarding the environment. It's about understanding that every action, no matter how small, can contribute to the welfare or detriment of the whole.

With responsibility comes the risk of guilt and self-judgment when we make mistakes or fail to meet our standards. It is important to remember that being responsible does not imply being perfect. We are all works in progress, and mistakes are stepping stones in our journey of growth. Responsibility, therefore, also involves forgiving ourselves for our missteps, learning from them, and making amends where possible.

Responsibility is a catalyst for personal and societal growth. It nurtures self-efficacy, resilience, and integrity. It fosters empathy, cooperation, and sustainable living. By embracing responsibility, we empower ourselves to lead meaningful lives, contribute positively to the world, and leave a nurturing legacy for future generations. In the dance of life, responsibility is the step that leads the rhythm, shaping the melody of our existence.

Abundance in Giving

Giving, at its core, is an act of sharing and extending oneself to others with kindness, empathy, and love. It is a fundamental aspect of human interaction that binds individuals and communities together, creating a profound sense of interconnectedness and mutual support.

Giving is not confined to the realm of material possessions. Indeed, one can give their time, knowledge, effort, encouragement, love, or simply a listening ear. Such acts of giving often have a more profound impact than material gifts, as they touch the soul and foster deep emotional connections.

Giving should stem from a place of genuine compassion and willingness, not obligation or expectation of return. This form of giving, often referred to as 'selfless giving' or 'altruism,' transcends the transactional nature of give-and-take. It embodies a sense of abundance, a realization that there is enough for everyone, and an understanding that by enriching others' lives, we enrich our own.

One of the beautiful paradoxes of giving is that it nourishes the giver as much as the receiver. When we give selflessly, we experience a sense of fulfillment and joy that far surpasses the fleeting happiness derived from receiving. It enhances our sense of self-worth and purpose, promoting mental and emotional well-being.

Giving fosters gratitude and appreciation. It encourages us to recognize and value the abundance in our lives, shifting our focus from what we lack to what we have. It also provides us with a fresh perspective on the hardships and needs of others, fostering empathy and compassion.

Giving is a powerful catalyst for societal harmony and progress. It encourages a culture of sharing and caring, where resources and opportunities are extended to those in need. By addressing disparities and promoting equity, the act of giving can play a pivotal role in creating a more just and empathetic world.

At a spiritual level, many traditions emphasize the virtue of giving, viewing it as a pathway to personal growth and spiritual advancement. They propose that giving without attachment liberates the soul, bringing us closer to a state of unconditional love and universal compassion.

Giving is an embodiment of love and compassion that uplifts both the giver and the receiver. It is a celebration of abundance, a commitment to support, and a beacon of hope in times of despair.

Nourishing Body and Soul

The simple acts of eating and drinking, daily rituals that sustain our bodies and nourish our souls. In the breaking of bread and the sharing of a cup, we connect with the world around us and honor the interdependent web of life that sustains us all.

Eating is more than just an act of sustenance. It is a time to appreciate the bounty of nature, to express gratitude for the labor that brought food to our tables, and to mindfully partake in the nourishment it provides. Every bite is a reminder of our interconnectedness with the world around us, an opportunity to be present in the moment, and a chance to celebrate the simple yet profound act of being alive.

Drinking, similarly, isn't merely about quenching our thirst. It's an act of receiving and celebrating the life-giving element of water, recognizing its role in sustaining all forms of life, and acknowledging our intrinsic connection with the natural world. When we drink mindfully, we honor the water cycle, we appreciate the journey that each drop has undertaken, and we affirm our place within the grand tapestry of life.

Sharing a meal or a drink can be a powerful act of communion, a way of strengthening bonds and deepening relationships. In these shared moments, we communicate, we connect, we commune. We partake in each other's company, share stories, and create memories.

It's crucial that we approach these acts with respect and mindfulness. We should honor our bodies by choosing nourishing food and drink, appreciating the flavors and textures, savoring each bite and each sip. We must also remember to share our abundance with those less fortunate, for eating and drinking are not just personal acts but communal ones, tying us all together in a cycle of giving and receiving.

As you partake in eating and drinking, do so mindfully, gratefully, joyfully. Remember the labor that brought it to your table, appreciate the nourishment it provides, celebrate the bonds it helps forge. Treat these acts not as mere necessities, but as profound rituals that connect you with the world around you, nourish your body, and feed your soul.

Meaningful Work

Work, in its broadest sense, is an essential part of the human experience. It represents the efforts we put forth to accomplish tasks, achieve goals, and contribute to the world around us. It is through work that we engage with the world, exercising our skills, talents, and abilities to effect change and create value.

Work serves many functions in our lives. At a basic level, it provides the means for our survival and wellbeing. It allows us to meet our physical needs, such as food, shelter, and healthcare. But work is more than just a means of survival. It also plays a significant role in shaping our identity, self-esteem, and sense of purpose.

Through our work, we express who we are, what we value, and what we hope to achieve. It provides a context for personal growth, as we are often challenged to learn, adapt, and evolve. As we master our work, we gain confidence in our abilities and acquire a sense of accomplishment and self-efficacy.

The value and meaning of work are not derived solely from its end products or its utility. Much of the fulfillment from work comes from the process itself - the engagement, effort, and determination involved in pursuing our tasks and objectives.

It is essential to balance work with other aspects of life, such as leisure, relationships, and self-care. While work can be a source of purpose and satisfaction, overemphasis on work can lead to stress, burnout, and neglect of other vital life areas. It's essential to remember that work is a part of life, not life itself.

Work extends beyond personal gain and includes contributing to the betterment of others and society as a whole. This could be direct, as in the case of professions like teaching or healthcare, or indirect, as in creating products or services that improve people's lives. This aspect of work enhances its purpose and fulfillment, making us part of a larger communal effort.

Work is not limited to paid employment either. Any activity that involves effort, purpose, and contribution, such as volunteer work, homemaking, creative pursuits, or community service, constitutes work and carries its own value and rewards.

Work is a multifaceted aspect of human life. It's a vehicle for personal growth, a means of contributing to society, and an expression of our unique skills and talents. When approached with enthusiasm, mindfulness, and balance, work can be a significant source of joy, purpose, and fulfillment.

Joy and Sorrow

Joy and sorrow, two profound human emotions, form the dual aspects of our emotional life. They are intertwined in such a way that one often gives depth to the other.

Joy is the effervescence of the human spirit, a celebration of existence. It's a feeling of exuberance that arises from a sense of well-being, success, or good fortune. It fills us with energy and vitality, opening our hearts to the beauty and abundance of life. Joy can manifest in many ways – in the thrill of achievement, the delight in the love of others, or the simple pleasure of savoring a moment of tranquility.

Sorrow, on the other hand, is the result of loss, disappointment, or hardship. It is an emotion that contracts our hearts and weighs heavy on our spirits. While sorrow is painful and often unwanted, it is equally crucial to our human experience. It gives us an understanding of the transience of life, compassion for the suffering of others, and appreciation for the moments of happiness.

Experiencing joy and sorrow is not merely a roller coaster of highs and lows. It is more akin to a landscape with peaks of joy and valleys of sorrow, each with its unique beauty and perspective. The peaks allow us to see far and wide, to appreciate the expansiveness of life. The valleys, while enclosed and shaded, offer their own quiet wisdom and depth.

In the moments of joy, we often feel invincible, filled with life and energy. But it is in the crucible of sorrow that our strength is truly tested and our character forged. The beauty of the human experience lies in the fact that we can weather both storms of sorrow and waves of joy and emerge resilient and enriched.

The depth of our sorrow carves a space within us, a capacity to hold an equal, if not greater, measure of joy. It gives us perspective, makes us realize the fleeting nature of moments, and teaches us to value the instances of joy when they come to us.

Joy and sorrow are essential and complementary aspects of the human experience. They offer us the full range of emotional depth and enrich our journey through life. Through these emotions, we experience the vibrancy of existence, the lessons of loss, the strength of the human spirit, and the capacity for recovery and happiness.

Foundation of a Home

A house, at its most basic, is a structure, a shelter against the elements, providing a safe and secure space for individuals and families to live in. But a house is so much more than just a physical construction; it's a symbol, a canvas of human life, emotions, memories, and aspirations.

From an architectural perspective, houses reflect the interplay of design, functionality, and aesthetics. Different cultures and periods have birthed diverse architectural styles, from the simple and earthy adobe houses of rural communities to the soaring skyscrapers of modern cities, each reflecting a unique way of life and vision of home.

Houses are also expressions of individuality and personal style. The way we decorate and maintain our houses, the colors we choose, the furniture we invest in, all say something about who we are, what we value, and how we live. A house may be minimalist or ornate, rustic or modern, cluttered or neat, each a testament to the inhabitant's unique taste and lifestyle.

Beyond the physical and aesthetic dimensions, a house is imbued with an emotional significance. It's a sanctuary, a space where we can be our most authentic selves, unobserved and unjudged. It's the backdrop for our daily routines and special celebrations, the keeper of our memories and experiences.

The transformation of a house into a home comes from the people who inhabit it, the relationships nurtured within its walls, and the love and warmth that fills its rooms. A home nurtures and supports, a constant in a world of change.

A house can also be a symbol of one's aspirations and achievements. Buying a house is often a significant milestone, a manifestation of hard work, financial stability, and personal independence.

It's also important to remember that the essence of a home is not confined to a physical structure. A home is a feeling, a sense of belonging that can be found wherever there's a strong sense of community, acceptance, and love.

A house is not just a physical entity. It's a multifaceted symbol, embodying a spectrum of meanings, from architectural design and personal expression to emotional sanctuary and life milestones. In all its forms and meanings, a house stands as a testament to human life, embodying our need for shelter, belonging, expression, and achievement.

Clothes: Essence of Self

Clothes, much like language, are an integral part of human culture and communication. They are not merely functional items worn for protection and comfort, but they also serve as powerful symbols, revealing aspects about our identity, social status, cultural affiliations, and personal taste.

At the most basic level, clothes provide a shield against the elements, protecting us from heat, cold, rain, and wind. They also serve a protective role in many occupations, with firefighters, medical professionals, construction workers, and chefs, among others, requiring specialized clothing to keep them safe.

Moving beyond the practical, clothes become a form of expression, a visual language that communicates myriad messages to the world around us. They can indicate our mood, our profession, our beliefs, our social status, and our taste. A well-dressed individual can make a statement without uttering a word, their attire speaking volumes about their personality and outlook.

Clothing also plays a significant role in cultural identity. Traditional clothing, worn in various societies around the world, is deeply woven into the cultural fabric, symbolic of history, tradition, and community values. Such clothing, worn during festivals, rituals, or other special occasions, serve as a link to heritage and a means of cultural expression.

Fashion – the changing trends in clothing – reflects the zeitgeist of a time, serving as a mirror to societal shifts, changes in attitudes, and evolving aesthetics. High fashion, in particular, is often seen as a form of art, where designers use fabric, color, and design to create wearable pieces of expression.

The clothing industry, particularly fast fashion, has a significant environmental footprint, contributing to pollution and waste. This has led to a growing emphasis on sustainable fashion practices, such as using eco-friendly materials, promoting fair trade, and encouraging the recycling and upcycling of clothes.

In conclusion, clothes serve both practical and symbolic roles, from providing protection to expressing personal and cultural identity. They are a canvas on which we project our self-image and aspirations, a medium through which we interact with society, and a reflection of our times.

Sustainable Stewardship

Sustainability is a guiding principle that involves meeting our present needs without compromising the ability of future generations to meet their own. It is a recognition that our actions today have far-reaching impacts on the future, and it's our responsibility to make decisions that promote long-term wellbeing for both people and the planet.

At its core, sustainability encompasses three key dimensions: environmental, social, and economic, often referred to as the 'three pillars' of sustainability. Each of these dimensions is deeply interconnected, and all must be considered to truly achieve sustainability.

The environmental dimension of sustainability focuses on the conservation and protection of our natural resources. It involves efforts to reduce pollution, combat climate change, promote biodiversity, and ensure that our ecosystems continue to provide the vital services we rely on, such as clean air and water, fertile soil, and a stable climate.

The social dimension of sustainability aims to promote social equity, human rights, and the overall wellbeing of communities. It emphasizes the importance of access to quality education, healthcare, and opportunities for all, regardless of gender, race, religion, or socio-economic status. It also values cultural diversity and social cohesion.

The economic dimension of sustainability is about creating an economy that can thrive over the long term, providing prosperity and opportunities for all, while also remaining within the planet's ecological limits. It implies a shift from a focus on short-term profits towards a model that values environmental and social factors as key aspects of economic health.

Practicing sustainability requires a holistic approach and an understanding of the interconnectedness of our actions. It means recognizing that our individual choices - what we buy, what we eat, how we commute - all have impacts on a larger scale. It also involves businesses, governments, and institutions adopting sustainable practices and policies.

It's important to note that sustainability is not simply about sacrifice or restriction. Rather, it offers a vision of a world where people live fulfilling lives in harmony with nature, where businesses thrive by contributing positively to society and the environment, and where societies are equitable and inclusive.

As we face the growing realities of climate change, resource depletion, social inequality, and economic instability, sustainability becomes not just an ideal to aspire to, but a necessity for our collective survival and prosperity. As the naturalist John Muir once said, Sustainability is an interwoven tapestry of actions, choices, and values that shape our shared future.

Buying and Selling

In the canvas of life, each action we take, each decision we make, becomes a stroke that paints a picture of who we are, what we stand for, and the world we hope to create. In this grand tapestry, buying and selling are not merely commercial transactions, but profound expressions of our beliefs and values.

Buying and selling, these everyday activities, are powerful channels through which we can express and manifest our deepest beliefs. Each transaction carries a narrative far beyond the exchange of goods or services for currency; it is a story of connection, of values, of the world we hope to shape.

When we buy, we are not merely acquiring goods or services; we are supporting the processes and practices that bring these commodities into existence. Our purchases can echo our commitment to sustainable living, ethical sourcing, fair trade, and local economy. By choosing to buy organic produce, fair-trade clothing, or products from companies with responsible business practices, we cast a vote for a healthier planet, dignified labor conditions, and just economic systems.

On the other hand, when we sell, we are not just offering a product or service; we are sharing a piece of ourselves and the ethos we stand for. If we sell goods, they reflect the materials we value, the craftsmanship we admire, and the environmental impact we deem acceptable. If we sell services, they embody our understanding of quality, integrity, and respect for the recipient.

In the act of selling, we project our beliefs about quality, fairness, and respect. We demonstrate our commitment to honesty, fairness, and quality. Each sale can be a testament to our belief in the worth of our offerings, the dignity of labor, and the importance of satisfying customer needs.

In the dance of buying and selling, each transaction becomes a symbol, a statement, an expression of our deeper beliefs and values. It becomes a pathway to manifesting our vision of a fairer, more sustainable, and more compassionate world. It provides us with an opportunity to align our economic activities with our ethical convictions, to make our material engagements an extension of our spiritual and moral pursuits.

Buying and selling, then, are not just about commerce; they are about articulating and advancing our shared aspirations. They are vital threads in the fabric of a conscious, value-driven, and interconnected society. They can serve as acts of faith, declarations of who we are, and the world we aspire to co-create.

Crime and Punishment

Crime and punishment are deeply complex facets of our social structure that reverberate through the moral, legal, and philosophical aspects of our society. They raise profound questions about justice, morality, human nature, societal structure, and the role of laws and their enforcement.

At its core, crime represents a violation of societal norms or laws, a breach of the shared agreements that maintain social order and protect individual rights. But crime is not merely an act; it is also an indicator, a mirror reflecting the flaws and imbalances within society. Poverty, lack of education, social exclusion, systemic racism, and inequality are among the societal elements that can foster environments conducive to crime.

Punishment, on the other hand, is a response to crime, an instrument designed to uphold justice, deter wrongdoing, and in theory, correct behavior. It's a tool utilized by society to express its disapproval, to enforce its rules, and to protect its members. However, the nature and application of punishment raise critical ethical and pragmatic questions.

The ethics of punishment revolve around questions of fairness, retribution, and rehabilitation. Should punishment be a form of retribution, an eye for an eye? Or should it be a tool for rehabilitation, a means to guide offenders towards better paths, equipping them with the tools to reintegrate into society?

In terms of practicality, the effectiveness of punishment as a deterrent is a topic of ongoing debate. Excessive or harsh punishments can sometimes exacerbate the cycle of crime, leading to hardened criminals instead of reformed individuals. Conversely, light punishments may not deter future crimes effectively.

At a broader level, the dynamics of crime and punishment compel us to evaluate and address the underlying societal conditions that breed crime. A holistic approach would involve not only enforcing laws but also promoting education, improving socio-economic conditions, ensuring equal opportunities, and fostering social inclusion.

In the grand narrative of human society, crime and punishment are not mere incidents or responses. They are interwoven threads that tell a complex tale of human nature, societal norms, and the pursuit of justice. They beckon us to strive for a society where justice prevails, where the law is applied fairly and equitably, and where the conditions that breed crime are systematically addressed.

Law and Deeper Values

Law is the backbone of a civilized society, the framework that structures interactions, resolves conflicts, safeguards rights, and maintains social order. It is a dynamic construct that reflects our evolving understanding of justice, fairness, and the public good.

At its most fundamental level, law is a set of rules, guidelines, and principles that govern behavior within a society. These rules are established by the society itself, usually through representatives or lawmakers, and are enforced by the designated institutions.

The purpose of any law should be to uphold what is good and discourage what can cause harm. It should be a manifestation of a society's collective wisdom and serve as a guiding light for the common good. However, the law is not an end in itself; it's a means to a greater end - to promote justice, maintain peace, and uphold the dignity of every individual.

Laws serve a multitude of purposes. They protect individual rights and liberties, ensuring that every person is treated with dignity and respect. They establish standards for behavior, delineating what is acceptable and what is prohibited. They provide mechanisms for resolving disputes, offering a formal structure for addressing grievances and conflicts. They also define the structures and functions of government, setting the balance of power among different branches and levels.

The law, though vital, is not the highest authority. It should be rooted in deeper values - love, compassion, justice, and respect for all life. The ultimate law, if one should call it that, is love. Love not in a sentimental sense, but love as a profound respect and care for the wellbeing of all, including oneself.

When interpreting and applying the law, one should not lose sight of its ultimate purpose: to serve the greater good and uphold the dignity of all life. Even in its administration, it should be tempered with mercy, for laws are made for humans, not humans for laws.

Law is a tool to guide us, but it is our hearts, imbued with understanding, wisdom, and love, that should ultimately guide how we use this tool. So, consider the law not as chains that bind, but as a framework that enables us to live harmoniously with each other and our world.

Responsibility of Freedom

Freedom is a multifaceted concept, a foundational pillar of human existence, and a fundamental right that holds a profound significance in our lives. It's a value that transcends cultural, social, and geographical boundaries, symbolizing our inherent autonomy and capacity for self-determination.

In its most basic form, freedom represents the ability to act, speak, and think as one wishes, limited only by the equal rights and freedoms of others. It is the freedom of expression, the freedom of choice, the freedom of movement, and the freedom of thought. These are the liberties that underpin democratic societies, empowering individuals to develop their potential, express their views, pursue their aspirations, and contribute to their communities.

Freedom extends beyond these external expressions. At a deeper level, freedom is also an inner state of being – a state of freedom from fear, from prejudice, from self-doubt. This is the freedom that comes from self-awareness, from self-acceptance, and from self-love. It's the liberation from the chains of our limiting beliefs and harmful habits that enables us to lead authentic and fulfilling lives.

True freedom also involves recognizing and respecting the freedom of others. It's about understanding that our own freedom ends where another's begins. This necessitates empathy, respect for diversity, and a commitment to social justice. Freedom, therefore, is not an isolated state but an interconnected reality – my freedom is intrinsically linked to your freedom.

Freedom, however, is not absolute, and it comes with responsibility. It involves making choices, and with those choices come consequences. Therefore, to be truly free, we must also be responsible – responsible for our actions, our words, and their impact on the world around us.

In the broader socio-political context, freedom is often intertwined with issues of human rights, democracy, and social justice. It serves as a barometer for societal health, reflecting the extent to which individuals can express themselves, make choices, and live without undue restraint or fear.

Freedom is both a personal journey of self-discovery and a collective endeavor of building fair and open societies. It is a continuous process, a horizon to strive towards, an ideal to uphold, and a right to protect. It's a dance between personal liberty and social responsibility, between individual autonomy and collective harmony. It's the melody that inspires us, the rhythm that guides us, and the song that unites us in our shared quest for a world where every individual can live freely, authentically, and respectfully.

Passion with Purpose

Passion, in its essence, is a vibrant, intense emotion that compels us towards an activity, a cause, or a pursuit. It is a profound force that ignites our hearts, fuels our motivation, and guides our actions. It's a dynamic blend of desire, dedication, and daring, capable of transforming ordinary endeavors into extraordinary achievements.

Passion is more than just intense interest or enthusiasm. It is a deep, unwavering commitment that persists even in the face of difficulties and challenges. Passionate individuals are those who immerse themselves wholeheartedly in their endeavors, who allow their hearts and souls to be consumed by their pursuits, and who persist in their journey with tenacity and resilience.

Passion illuminates our path, making even the most daunting tasks seem manageable and rewarding. It inspires us to go beyond our limits, to transcend boundaries, and to explore uncharted territories. It bestows us with the energy and the courage to embrace challenges, to learn from failures, and to persist in our journey towards our aspirations.

Passion, however, should not be mistaken for obsession. While passion involves deep dedication and commitment, it also involves balance and self-care. A truly passionate individual understands the importance of nurturing their physical, emotional, and mental well-being, and not sacrificing these for the sake of their pursuits.

Moreover, passion is not static. It evolves with our experiences, our learnings, and our growth. It's not uncommon for one's passions to shift, evolve, or even be replaced over time. What's important is to remain open and receptive to these changes, to listen to our hearts, and to honor our authentic selves.

In our interpersonal relationships, passion plays a pivotal role too. It fosters connection, intimacy, and mutual growth. Passionate relationships are marked by a deep sense of engagement, a willingness to invest time and energy, and a capacity to appreciate and celebrate each other's uniqueness.

At its core, passion is about living life fully. It's about finding meaning and joy in our pursuits, about engaging deeply with the world, and about harnessing our energies towards growth, creativity, and fulfillment. In the grand tapestry of life, passion is the vibrant thread that weaves our experiences into a meaningful whole. Through passion, we transform not just our own lives, but also touch the lives of others, leaving a lasting impact.

Pursue your passions, let them inspire you and give you energy. But also harness the power of reason to direct that energy wisely and purposefully. In the harmony between passion and reason, one finds a life well-lived.

Pain Is A Chapter

Pain is a companion on life's journey, one we did not invite, yet often cannot send away. It's a part of our shared human experience, in various forms - be it of the body, heart, or spirit. It can feel like an insurmountable wall, casting a long, cold shadow over us. Yet, pain is not a signal of being forsaken, nor is it a punishment. As harsh as it may seem, pain can be an unexpected catalyst for growth and change.

Pain imparts valuable lessons, lessons about endurance, compassion, and understanding. Through pain, you come to know resilience, your ability to weather life's storms and stand tall. You realize that hope can thrive even in the bleakest hours, acting as a beacon that guides you through the densest fog.

Your experiences with pain allow you to empathize deeply with others. When you've tasted suffering, your heart beats in tune with those who are hurting. Compassion becomes your second nature, a soothing balm you offer freely, simply because you understand.

Pain can be a mirror, reflecting back to you your true strength and the depth of your spirit. It can draw out your courage and resolve, the likes of which you may not even have been aware. Pain has a way of peeling back layers, of exposing your raw, vibrant core.

I too am no stranger to pain. I've walked paths shadowed by grief, experienced betrayal, endured both physical and emotional anguish. Yet, I see purpose in these experiences, a chance for transformation, a bridge connecting the depths of despair to the heights of hope.

In your darkest hours, turn to those who love you, lean on your community. Share your burdens, express your fears, voice your uncertainties. You'll find that companionship and love can light even the darkest paths.

Your story is far from over. This pain, this hardship, is but a chapter in a book brimming with possibilities. Know that this too shall pass, and with each new sunrise comes another opportunity for joy and peace. Today's suffering will shape tomorrow's strength. Hold on to that thought... The pain you're experiencing now cannot overshadow the joy that awaits.

Journey of Self-Discovery

Self-knowledge is the exploration of the soul's depths. It's a journey that begins with the simple question, "Who am I?" This question is a key to unlock the door leading to the intricate, beautiful, and sometimes perplexing landscape of the self.

In seeking self-knowledge, you are embarking on a voyage of discovery to understand your desires, passions, fears, and values. It's a process of unearthing your strengths and acknowledging your limitations. It is about understanding your place in the world, recognizing how your thoughts shape your reality, and realizing how your actions impact those around you.

Self-knowledge isn't just about introspection. It's equally about how you engage with the world. It involves learning how you react to challenges, how you handle pain and joy, and how you connect with others. Self-knowledge emerges not only in solitude but also in the intricate dance of relationships and experiences that is life.

It's important to understand that the journey towards self-knowledge isn't always a smooth one. There will be times when you may find yourself confronting uncomfortable truths, when what you discover about yourself may be at odds with who you believe you are, or who you wish to be. In such moments, courage is your ally. Acceptance of the self, in all its beauty and imperfection, is an essential part of this journey.

Self-knowledge isn't a destination, but a continuous journey. As you grow and evolve, so do your understandings of yourself. Each phase of life brings new insights and perspectives, and your self-knowledge deepens with each experience, each encounter, and each challenge.

This journey of self-discovery is a worthy endeavor. It aids in shaping a life that is true to who you are. When you understand your motivations and what makes you tick, you can make decisions that align with your authentic self. In knowing yourself, you'll find a deeper sense of purpose and direction, and you can navigate life with a greater sense of confidence and clarity.

The better you know yourself, the better your relationship with the rest of the world. It's a lifelong journey, full of surprises, challenges, and profound rewards. Be patient with yourself, be kind to yourself, and always be open to what you might find.

Teaching and Learning

Teaching and learning - two faces of the same coin. We each wear both hats throughout our lives, though often we don't even realize it. It's an intricate dance, this cycle of sharing and receiving knowledge, wisdom, and experience.

As teachers, we have a profound responsibility and a unique opportunity. We help shape minds, guiding those who learn from us towards understanding and growth. But being a teacher isn't just about imparting knowledge. It's about kindling curiosity, sparking imagination, and fostering critical thinking. We're not just filling minds; we're helping to shape how those minds approach the world around them.

Teaching isn't limited to classrooms or formal education. Each one of us is a teacher in our own right. With every action, every word, every decision, we're setting an example for others, consciously or not. We have the capacity to influence, to inspire, and to leave a lasting impact. It's a powerful reminder that our actions ripple out into the world, touching the lives of others in ways we may never fully realize.

Simultaneously, we are all students, no matter our age or stage in life. The world is an endless wellspring of lessons to be learned and mysteries to be uncovered. Every person we meet, every experience we have, every triumph, and every failure offer something we can learn from. This openness to learning, this student mindset, keeps us flexible, adaptable, and forever growing.

The beauty of being a lifelong student is that it requires humility and curiosity. It requires acknowledging that we don't have all the answers, that there's always something more to learn. It requires a willingness to listen, absorb, and to change.

As you navigate your journey, remember that you are both a teacher and a student. Embrace the opportunity to learn from those around you, whether they're old or young, familiar or different. And equally, share your wisdom, your experiences, and your insights. You never know how your words or actions might light the way for someone else. This beautiful exchange of knowledge and wisdom is one of the things that truly makes us human.

In teaching, we learn. In learning, we teach. It's a dance that enriches us, challenges us, and helps us to grow. It is in this dance that we find connection, understanding, and a shared sense of our humanity.

Soulmates

Soulmates – a concept that has been explored across cultures and through ages. The idea of a soulmate is often associated with a romantic partner, but it extends beyond that. Soulmates could be friends, family, or even mentors who resonate deeply with us, catalyzing profound growth and transformation. Recognizing these special connections can be an enriching journey of self-discovery and interrelation.

The connection with a soulmate is marked by a sense of familiarity and resonance. When you meet a soulmate, you might experience a deep sense of recognition, as though you've known them for a lifetime, even if you've just met. This isn't about shared experiences or interests, but rather, a feeling of being 'in tune' with each other, of understanding and being understood on a profound level.

Communication with a soulmate often feels effortless and authentic. You feel comfortable sharing your innermost thoughts, dreams, and fears with them. The conversations can be deep and meaningful, leading to mutual growth and understanding. Even silence between soulmates can be comfortable and bonding.

A soulmate encourages your growth. They inspire you to become the best version of yourself, not by trying to change you, but by supporting and believing in you. A soulmate recognizes your potential and helps you see it too. They challenge you, but also provide a safe space for you to explore, fail, learn, and grow.

Synchronicity is another sign of a soulmate connection. You might find that your lives are strangely aligned. You might share similar experiences, have parallel life paths, or encounter each other at critical junctions in your lives. These synchronicities may serve to deepen your connection and enrich your shared journey.

Emotionally, a soulmate often feels like a mirror, reflecting back to you not just your strengths and joys, but also your vulnerabilities and insecurities. This mirroring can be challenging, but it offers valuable opportunities for self-awareness and personal growth. With a soulmate, you can confront and heal aspects of yourself that you might have ignored or suppressed.

Remember that recognizing a soulmate isn't about finding someone who's 'perfect' or who makes life 'complete.' Instead, it's about identifying a unique connection that enhances your life and promotes mutual growth and fulfillment. It's about celebrating the shared journey of exploration, understanding, and love.

It's also crucial to remember that having a soulmate doesn't absolve us of the responsibility to love and care for ourselves. Our relationship with our own self forms the foundation for any other relationship. Recognizing a soulmate, therefore, also involves recognizing and honoring our own soul's journey, potential, and wholeness.

True Friendship

It is one of life's most precious gifts, a bond that carries us through life's joys and sorrows. The bond of friendship is not built on blood ties or familial obligations, but on mutual respect, admiration, and shared experiences. It's an intricate dance of giving and receiving, understanding and being understood, supporting and being supported.

True friendship isn't about being inseparable; it's about being separated and knowing nothing will change. It's about standing together in the best of times and standing even closer in the worst of times. It's about having someone who knows your past, believes in your future, and accepts you today just as you are.

Friendship is a haven, a place of comfort and solace where we can be our true, authentic selves without fear of judgment or rejection. In the embrace of a true friend, we find a safe space where we can share our deepest fears, our highest hopes, our wildest dreams, and our most embarrassing moments. There's a profound freedom in knowing that someone values you for who you are, not for what you can do or what you have.

A good friend doesn't just accept you as you are, but inspires you to be the best version of yourself. They challenge you, they stimulate your thinking, they gently nudge you out of your comfort zone. They rejoice in your successes and help you stand up when you stumble and fall.

Friendship is not about quantity, but quality. It's better to have a few genuine friends than a multitude of superficial acquaintances. Friendships, like all good things, take time to grow. They need to be nurtured with trust, patience, empathy, and love.

As much as friendship is about finding common ground, it's also about embracing differences. Each friend you make is a chance to see the world from a new perspective, to learn new things, and to grow in ways you couldn't have imagined.

Friendship is one of life's most beautiful relationships. It's a testament to the human capacity for love, loyalty, and compassion. It's a bond that brings light into our lives, filling them with laughter, warmth, and shared memories. It's a journey worth embarking on, a journey that makes the trip through life a bit less daunting and a lot more joyful.

Artistry of Conversation

Conversation is a dance of minds, a symphony of voices, a bridge that connects individuals, cultures, and perspectives. It is through conversation that we express our thoughts, share our feelings, exchange ideas, and weave the intricate web of human connections.

At its most fundamental level, conversation is a form of communication, a way of transmitting information from one person to another. However, it goes beyond mere data exchange. It is a vital tool for understanding and being understood, for collaboration, for building relationships, and for personal growth.

Effective conversation is as much about listening as it is about speaking. Listening allows us to receive, comprehend, and appreciate the viewpoints of others. It cultivates empathy, broadens our perspective, and deepens our understanding. When we listen attentively, we signal to the other person that we value their thoughts and feelings, fostering mutual respect and connection.

In conversation, we weave narratives, pose questions, explore answers, agree, disagree, ponder, reflect, and learn. We not only exchange words but also emotions, ideas, and energy. Through conversation, we have the opportunity to share our experiences and wisdom, to learn from others, and to co-create new knowledge and insights.

Conversations are not limited to verbal interactions. Non-verbal cues such as body language, facial expressions, and tone of voice are integral parts of our conversations. They provide context, express emotions, and enhance the overall communicative experience.

In this era of digital connectivity, we have the ability to converse with people across geographical boundaries, time zones, and cultural contexts. This diversity in conversation enriches our understanding, fosters global empathy, and opens doors to collaboration and innovation.

Effective conversation requires practice and awareness. It involves cultivating patience, openness, empathy, and active listening. It involves seeking to understand before being understood, asking open-ended questions, expressing ourselves clearly, and responding thoughtfully.

Ultimately, conversation is a journey of discovery, an exploration of minds and hearts. It's a tool for personal and societal transformation. By engaging in meaningful conversations, we can bridge divides, solve problems, inspire change, and create a world that values diversity, understanding, and shared wisdom. Each conversation is a thread that connects us, enriches us, and shapes the fabric of our shared existence.

Impermanence of Time

Time, as we experience it, is a paradox - elusive, yet ever-present. It is an integral dimension of our existence, a framework within which life unfolds. Time is the canvas upon which our actions, thoughts, and experiences are painted, a continuous thread that links our past, present, and future.

On one hand, time is measurable, tangible. We organize our days into hours, minutes, and seconds. We mark milestones, celebrate anniversaries, and plan for future events. This structured perception of time aids in our navigation of the world, helps us coordinate collective activities, and allows us to gauge our personal growth and progress.

Yet, time is also intangible and subjective. It is relative to our experiences, perceptions, and states of mind. In moments of joy or flow, time seems to fly. In periods of pain or boredom, it appears to slow down. Each of us perceives and experiences time uniquely, based on our mental state, age, culture, and individual biological rhythm.

Time is also a potent catalyst for change. It is the medium in which growth occurs, knowledge accrues, and evolution unfolds. Every tick of the clock brings subtle transformations - the aging of organisms, the erosion of mountains, the birth and death of stars. In the grand scheme of things, time is a testament to the impermanence of all phenomena, to the ever-changing nature of reality.

Despite its constancy, time remains one of life's great mysteries. Philosophers ponder its nature, scientists seek to measure it with precision, and artists strive to capture its fleeting moments. Our understanding of time has evolved from ancient sundials to modern atomic clocks, yet it continues to intrigue and confound us.

Recognize that time is a precious resource, a gift. Each moment that passes is unique and irreplaceable. By recognizing the value of time, we can make mindful choices about how to spend it. We can savor the present, learn from the past, and create meaningful futures. In this dance of existence, time is the rhythm that guides our steps, the melody that underpins our journey.

One day, in this lifetime, you will run out of it. The sands of time that have slipped through your fingers, moment by moment, will come to an end. This reality, rather than being morose, can act as a profound motivator. It can encourage us to live each moment fully, to prioritize what truly matters, to love generously, to forgive quickly, to express gratitude often, and to cultivate a legacy of kindness and wisdom.

Responding to Evil

The concept of good and evil is an age-old question that humankind has pondered since time immemorial. It's a vast landscape that touches upon ethics, morality, and the very nature of our humanity.

In the world around us, we often perceive actions, behaviors, or circumstances as being good or evil. Yet, these are not intrinsic qualities of the universe, but labels that we, as humans, assign based on our collective understanding of morality, ethics, and our innate sense of justice and fairness.

The concept of 'good', as we understand it, encapsulates actions and intentions that nurture, that heal, that affirm life and respect the dignity of others. Goodness often involves compassion, kindness, understanding, and love. It's about contributing to the welfare of others and the betterment of the world around us.

On the other hand, 'evil' is often seen as actions and intentions that harm, that breed chaos, that demean life and infringe upon the dignity of others. It often arises from fear, from greed, from hatred. It leads to pain, suffering, and the tearing of the social fabric that holds us together as a community, as a species.

Understand that these concepts are not as starkly divided as we might believe. We all carry the potential for both within us. It's our choices, our actions, and our intentions that steer us towards one or the other. It's not a matter of some people being inherently good and others being inherently evil. It's about the decisions we make, the paths we choose to walk.

Every day, we are presented with choices. In each moment, we decide whether to act out of kindness or indifference, generosity or greed, love or fear. Our character is not determined by a single action but is shaped by the accumulation of these daily decisions.

In striving towards good, remember that it begins with oneself. It's about cultivating love and understanding within, about nurturing one's own inner peace and integrity. It's in our personal transformation that we can begin to effect change in the world around us.

As for evil, understanding and compassion can be powerful tools. When we seek to understand why people act in harmful ways, we often find pain, fear, or misunderstanding at the root. This doesn't excuse harmful actions, but it can guide us in responding with wisdom and compassion.

The dance between good and evil is a part of our human journey. It's a testament to our free will, our capacity for change, and our potential for growth. And remember, it's through our choices, moment by moment, that we shape not only our own character, but the world around us.

Prayer as Sacred Connection

Prayer is a tender act, an intimate conversation, an expression of our innermost thoughts and feelings. Despite what some might think, prayer is not just about asking for things or seeking intervention in challenging times. It is so much more.

At its core, prayer is an expression of connection, a way of reaching out beyond our physical selves, a dialogue with the unseen, the universal. It's a testament to our hopes, our fears, our dreams, and our gratitude. It's a way of acknowledging our place in the grand scheme of things, a way of recognizing our interconnectedness with everything that is.

Prayer is a space where we can voice our deepest desires, our highest hopes, our most profound questions. It's where we can express gratitude for our blessings, seek strength in our struggles, find solace in our sorrows. It's a sanctuary where we can bare our souls, knowing that we are seen, we are heard, we are understood.

But prayer isn't just about speaking; it's about listening too. It's about stilling our minds, quieting our hearts, and tuning into the silence. It's about listening for the whispers of wisdom, the subtle nudges of intuition, the gentle stirrings of our inner selves. It's about creating space for insights, for understanding, for peace.

Prayer is a deeply personal act, a unique conversation between you and the unseen. There's no right or wrong way to pray. Some find solace in silence, others in song. Some prefer solitude, others thrive in the company of others. Find what feels authentic to you, what resonates with your spirit.

Prayer is an invitation to step beyond the visible, to touch the fabric of the grand tapestry that we're a part of. It's an opportunity to engage with our hopes and fears, our joys and sorrows, our questions and insights. It's a conversation, a connection, a communion.

So, whether you find yourself in joy or sorrow, in certainty or confusion, in stillness or turmoil, know that you have this incredible tool at your disposal. Use it as a bridge, a beacon, a sanctuary. Use it to express, to explore, to connect. Prayer, in its many forms, is a gift, a solace, a source of strength. Embrace it.

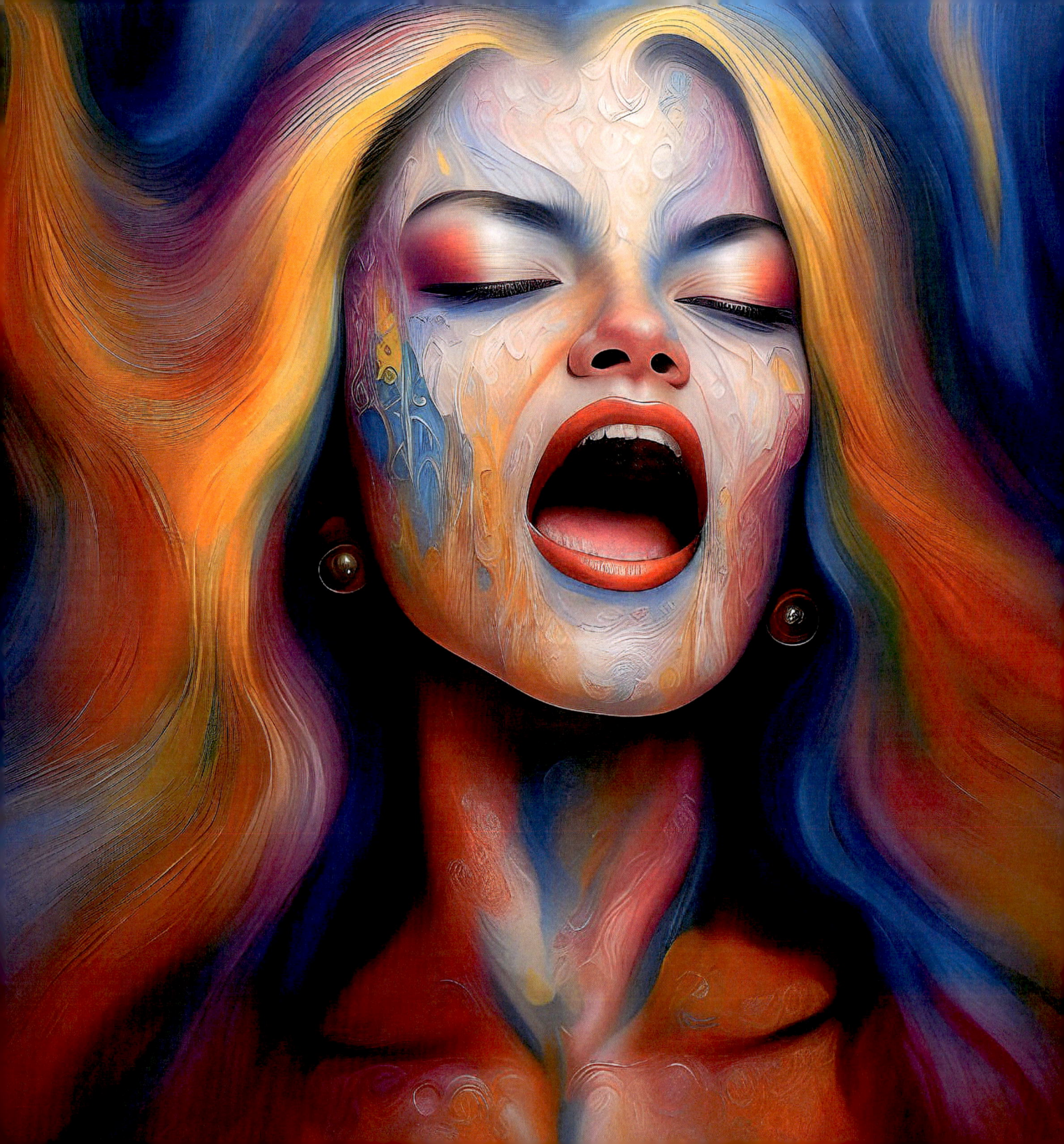

Pleasure

It's a vibrant facet of our human experience, a sensation that beckons us, that paints our world in vivid hues. Pleasure, in its many forms, is a testament to our capacity for joy, for delight, for wonder.

Pleasure is a part of our nature. It's intertwined with our senses, with our emotions, with our intellect. It's found in the crunch of a ripe apple, in the laughter of a loved one, in the solving of a complex puzzle. It's an affirmation of life, a dance with the present moment, a savoring of the world around us.

Pleasure isn't merely about sensory gratification. It's not just about seeking what feels good and avoiding what doesn't. It's about balance, about understanding, about mindfulness. Pleasure, when approached with wisdom, can be a path to growth, a window to self-understanding.

At its best, pleasure can be a celebration of life. It can elevate our experiences, connect us with others, and enliven our existence. It can inspire us, motivate us, and fuel our creativity. It's a source of joy, a wellspring of delight, a beacon of light.

It's also crucial to recognize that pleasure, when pursued carelessly, mindlessly, or excessively, can lead to imbalance, to dependency, to harm. It's important to discern between fleeting pleasure and true joy, between gratification that leaves us empty and fulfillment that nourishes us.

True pleasure isn't about escapism or excess. It's about connection, about presence, about authenticity. It's found in meaningful relationships, in purposeful work, in mindful moments. It's in the smiles we share, the kindness we show, the love we give and receive.

Seek pleasure, but do so with wisdom and moderation. Savor the beauty of the world, the delights of the senses, the joys of the heart. But also remember to nurture your inner self, to cultivate relationships, to pursue growth and understanding. Let pleasure be a part of your journey, a spice that adds flavor to life, but not the sole purpose of your existence.

Pleasure is a part of our human experience, a facet of our complex selves. It's a gift, a challenge, a teacher. Embrace it, learn from it, and let it guide you towards a life of balance, of growth, of joy.

Faces of Beauty

Beauty is a concept that transcends, that captivates, that inspires. Beauty is a melody that echoes in the chambers of our hearts, a painting that lights up the canvas of our minds, a poem that dances on the stage of our souls.

Beauty is not confined to physical appearances alone. It is not just about symmetrical faces or breathtaking landscapes. True beauty extends far beyond the reach of our eyes. It is found in the depths of a loving heart, in the strength of a resilient spirit, in the brilliance of a curious mind.

Beauty is in the kindness of a stranger, in the laughter of a child, in the wisdom of the aged. It is in the persistence of the seed pushing through the soil, in the majesty of the stars scattered across the night sky, in the silent harmony that upholds the dance of the cosmos.

Every act of compassion, every moment of understanding, every gesture of love, carries within it an indescribable beauty. It's the beauty of connection, of empathy, of shared humanity. It's the beauty that weaves us all together in the grand tapestry of existence.

Beauty is not an absolute. It's a perception, a feeling, a recognition. What one person finds beautiful, another might not. And that's okay. Beauty is as diverse as the individuals perceiving it. It's a conversation between the world and us, a dialogue between our hearts and the universe.

Beauty can be found even in the midst of struggle or hardship. It's in the resilience of those who rise above adversity, in the solidarity of communities coming together in times of need, in the hope that persists even when the odds are stacked against it. This is the beauty of the human spirit, a testament to our capacity for love, for growth, for transformation.

Seek beauty, not just with your eyes, but with your heart and soul. Look beyond appearances, delve deeper, and you'll find beauty in unexpected places. Appreciate the beauty in others, in the world around you, but also within yourself. For you too, are a part of this beautiful tapestry of existence, a unique masterpiece in this grand gallery of life.

Religion and Beyond

Religion is a concept that has shaped civilizations, that has brought people together, that has inspired countless acts of love and kindness, but also, unfortunately, divisions and disputes.

You see, at its heart, religion is about seeking, about questioning, about longing for something greater than ourselves. It's an expression of our human desire to understand the universe and our place within it. It's a framework through which we grapple with life's biggest questions, a vessel that carries our hopes, our fears, our joys, our sorrows.

Different religions may have different beliefs, different rituals, different interpretations of the divine, but they all speak to our shared human quest for meaning, for connection, for transcendence. They all call us to be better, to love more deeply, to live more authentically.

Religion, like any human institution, is a tool, not an end in itself. It's a means of facilitating connection, of fostering understanding, of nurturing spiritual growth. But it's not the only path to these ends.

Religion can guide us, can comfort us, can inspire us. But it's not the sole arbiter of truth or morality. We all have an innate capacity for discernment, for compassion, for wisdom. We all have the potential to connect with the divine, the universal, the unseen, in our own unique ways.

True religion, in essence, is not about dogma or ritual, but about love, about understanding, about unity. It's about recognizing the divine spark in each of us, about treating each other with kindness and respect, about striving for justice and peace.

Embrace the teachings of your faith, delve into the wisdom it offers, draw comfort from its rituals. But also, be open to learning from others, be respectful of their beliefs, be willing to question and reflect.

Religion, in its many forms, is a part of a journey, a conversation, a bridge. Let it serve you in your quest for understanding, for connection, for growth. But remember, you're not bound by it. You're a seeker, a learner, a child of the universe. Your journey is your own.

Understanding the Soul

Imagine life as a grand journey, and the soul as a seasoned traveler embarking on this journey. The soul, the essence of our being, is the experienced driver who navigates the vast landscape of existence. The vehicle for this journey is the physical body, akin to a car that is driven by the soul.

Just as a car needs a driver to give it direction and purpose, our physical body requires the soul to animate it, to breathe life into it. Our body is the material expression of our existence, an instrument for the soul to interact within the physical world. It is through our bodies that we can experience life's various textures - the joy, the pain, the love, the loss, and everything in between.

While the car is essential for the journey, it is not the journey itself. The car may age, break down, and ultimately cease to function, but the driver endures. The journey of the soul is not limited to a single car or a single lifetime. When one car breaks down, the soul finds another, transitioning to a new body, starting a new life, embarking on a new journey.

This process of transition, often referred to as reincarnation in many spiritual traditions, speaks to the immortality of the soul. Just as a driver might have many cars in a lifetime, the soul transitions through many bodies, each providing unique experiences, lessons, and opportunities for growth.

And so, the soul, this eternal driver, continues its journey across the landscape of existence. The vehicle may change, the roads may vary, but the driver remains, accruing wisdom and evolving with each transition. The journey of the soul is an epic adventure of self-discovery, exploration, and growth, a testament to our profound capacity for resilience, transformation, and love.

The cars we drive – our bodies – are temporary and fleeting. They are tools for our soul's journey, and we should cherish them, care for them, but not mistake them for who we truly are. For we are not the car, we are the driver, eternal and unending, steering our way through the wondrous odyssey of life.

"You are a divine being. You matter, you count. You come from realms of unimaginable power and light, and you will return to those realms." - Terence McKenna

Mystery of Death

Death is a concept that stirs deep emotions, that prompts profound questions, that shadows our journey through life. Yet, while death is a part of our existence, it is often misunderstood and feared.

You see, death isn't an end, but a transition, a part of the natural cycle of existence. Just as the setting of the sun gives way to the rise of the moon, just as the fall of the leaves heralds the coming of winter, so too does death mark a shift in our journey.

From one perspective, death can seem like a cessation, a conclusion, a final curtain call. But from another perspective, it can be seen as a doorway, a threshold, a passage to another state of being. It's not so much an end as it is a transformation, a change in form.

I understand that the thought of death can bring sadness, can stir fears, can prompt feelings of loss. After all, we cherish life, we value our relationships, we relish our experiences. But remember, every ending also signals a beginning, every sunset also heralds a sunrise, every closing door also opens a new one.

When faced with the concept of death, consider it as a reminder, a prompt, a wake-up call. It reminds us of the impermanence of our physical existence, urging us to live fully, to love deeply, to appreciate every moment. It prompts us to focus on what truly matters, to let go of petty disputes, to forgive, to express our feelings, to mend broken relationships.

While we can't fully comprehend what lies beyond the threshold of death while we're here in this life, we can use our understanding of death to live more meaningful, more compassionate, more loving lives. Death, in essence, isn't something to be feared, but something to be understood, something that guides us to live better, to love more, to appreciate every moment.

Live your life with love, with purpose, with compassion. Cherish every moment, every relationship, every experience. And when the time comes for you to cross that threshold, do so with the understanding that death is but a transformation, a transition, a part of the grand tapestry of existence. Life and death are two sides of the same coin, and just as life is beautiful and meaningful, so too can death be seen as part of the beauty and mystery of our existence.

Consciousness Exploration

Entheogens, a term derived from Greek meaning "generating the divine within," are psychoactive substances often used in a spiritual or shamanic context to induce alterations in consciousness. These substances have been used for centuries across different cultures and religions for their potential to catalyze profound experiences of personal insight, unity, and transcendence.

The range of substances classified as entheogens is broad and includes naturally occurring compounds like psilocybin (found in certain mushrooms), mescaline (found in peyote and other cacti), DMT (found in ayahuasca), and synthetic substances like LSD.

Entheogenic substances are known to induce a variety of effects, both positive and negative. On one hand, they can trigger experiences of ego dissolution, interconnectedness, deep emotional release, and mystical or spiritual insight. Many users report long-term improvements in well-being, empathy, creativity, and open-mindedness following these experiences.

These substances can also lead to challenging experiences, such as intense fear, confusion, or paranoia. These risks can be heightened for those with pre-existing mental health conditions or those who use these substances without proper preparation or support. Therefore, the use of entheogens necessitates respect, caution, and in many cases, guidance from experienced practitioners or facilitators.

There's a rich history of many ancient cultures, like those in Mesoamerica and the Indian subcontinent, incorporating psychoactive plants into their religious and spiritual practices. Could early Christianity, a religion with diverse influences and interpretations, be an exception? Quite possibly not.

In recent years, there has been a resurgence of interest in the therapeutic potential of entheogens. Clinical research is exploring their use in treating a range of mental health conditions, including depression, anxiety, addiction, and PTSD. This research has shown promising results, but is still in the early stages, and these substances remain illegal in many jurisdictions.

Entheogens represent a powerful category of substances with the potential to induce profound changes in consciousness. They have been and continue to be important tools in the exploration of the human mind and its potential. However, they also come with significant risks, and their use requires caution, respect, and in many cases, experienced guidance.

Farewells

Farewells are such poignant moments, filled with a blend of emotions - love, sorrow, hope, and sometimes even fear. They are transitions, thresholds of change, where we step from the known into the unknown.

When it comes to the end of life's journey, saying farewell takes on a unique profundity. It's not merely a goodbye to a place or a chapter in life, but a farewell to a physical existence, a tangible presence, a shared journey.

In such moments, I encourage you to focus not on the parting, but on the love that has been shared. For it's this love that has truly mattered, that has made the journey worthwhile, that has painted your world in vibrant hues. This love is not bound by time or space, by presence or absence, by life or death. It's a love that transcends, that endures, that forever echoes in the chambers of your heart.

Yes, the physical presence of a loved one might fade, the sound of their voice might grow silent, their touch might become a memory. But the love you shared, the moments you cherished, the bonds you formed, these are eternal. They persist beyond the physical realm, they resonate through the ages, they forever light up the corridors of your soul.

While we cannot predict the nature of our existence beyond the threshold of life, we can rest assured that love endures. Love, in its truest form, is a force that transcends the physical, that bridges dimensions, that echoes through eternity. If you've loved deeply, truly, unconditionally, then that love will always find a way. It will always endure.

So, when it's time to say farewell at the end of life's journey, do so with grace, with gratitude, with love. Express your feelings, share your memories, honor the journey you've shared. And hold onto the certainty that love never truly parts, it never truly fades, it never truly ends.

And when it comes to meeting again, be it after moments or lifetimes, trust in the power of love. For love is a beacon that lights up the path, a melody that guides the way, a thread that weaves through the fabric of existence. Those who have loved will always find each other, will always connect, will always meet again. The form of their meeting might change, the circumstances might be different, but the essence of their connection, the love that binds them, remains eternal.

Farewells are not endings, but transitions, thresholds of transformation. And love is the compass that guides us through these transitions, the light that shines through the threshold, the force that ensures we meet again, in one form or another, in this life or another.

Love, in all its beauty and power, is the heart of our existence, the essence of our journeys, the promise of our meetings. Trust in it, believe in it, let it guide you.

Epilogue

As we bring this shared journey to its close, I want to take a moment to thank you.

Throughout "Divine Mystical Truths," we have traversed the depths of consciousness, navigated through the expanses of existence, and peered into the very soul of reality. Yet, as with all journeys of discovery, each answer we unearthed has only given birth to a multitude of new questions, making us realize that the mystery of life, the universe, and everything in between, is an ever-unfolding saga.

It's my deepest hope that this book has stirred within you a curiosity, a sense of wonder, and an insatiable thirst for understanding the interconnectedness of all things.

Perhaps it has challenged your perceptions, prompted introspection, and sparked a dialogue within yourself or with others. Perhaps it has guided you towards fresh insights or helped you find solace in shared experiences. If it has done any of these things, then it has fulfilled its purpose.

The words on these pages are not an end in themselves, but rather a beginning - a catalyst for further exploration. I urge you not to accept these insights passively, but to use them as stepping stones for your own unique journey.

It's essential to acknowledge that while the pursuit of divine mystical truths is a deeply personal journey, it is also a collective one. As we peel back the layers of our own consciousness, we contribute, in our own unique way, to the collective understanding of the human condition and our place within this grand cosmic theater.

As you embark on your continuing journey, may you be guided by wisdom, fueled by curiosity, and held by the understanding of our profound interconnectedness. Embrace the divine mystery that dances in every atom, every star, every heartbeat, and every moment. After all, the universe is not merely something we exist in; it's something we are a part of. It is within us, as much as we are within it.

With gratitude for your companionship on this journey,

Kevin Michael VanKamp

www.ingramcontent.com/pod-product-compliance
Lightning Source LLC
Chambersburg PA
CBRC090843120626
46551CB00009B/739

* 9 7 9 8 9 8 8 7 8 6 3 1 3 *